Security Leader Insights for Success

Security Leader Insights for Success

Lessons and Strategies from Leading Security Professionals

Dave Komendat, Contributing Editor

ELSEVIER

AMSTERDAM • BOSTON • HEIDELBERG • LONDON
NEW YORK • OXFORD • PARIS • SAN DIEGO
SAN FRANCISCO • SINGAPORE • SYDNEY • TOKYO

Security
Executive Council

Elsevier
225 Wyman Street, Waltham, MA 02451, USA
The Boulevard, Langford Lane, Kidlington, Oxford, OX5 1GB, UK

Notices

Knowledge and best practice in this field are constantly changing. As new research and experience broaden our understanding, changes in research methods, professional practices, or medical treatment may become necessary.

Practitioners and researchers must always rely on their own experience and knowledge in evaluating and using any information, methods, compounds, or experiments described herein. In using such information or methods they should be mindful of their own safety and the safety of others, including parties for whom they have a professional responsibility.

To the fullest extent of the law, neither the Publisher nor the authors, contributors, or editors, assume any liability for any injury and/or damage to persons or property as a matter of products liability, negligence or otherwise, or from any use or operation of any methods, products, instructions, or ideas contained in the material herein.

Library of Congress Cataloging-in-Publication Data
A catalog record for this book is available from the Library of Congress

British Library Cataloguing in Publication Data
A catalogue record for this book is available from the British Library

ISBN: 978-0-12-800844-7

For more publications in the Elsevier Risk Management and Security Collection, visit our website at store.elsevier.com/SecurityExecutiveCouncil.

This book has been manufactured using Print On Demand technology. Each copy is produced to order and is limited to black ink. The online version of this book will show color figures where appropriate.

Working together
to grow libraries in
developing countries

ELSEVIER Book Aid International

www.elsevier.com • www.bookaid.org

CONTENTS

Experienced corporate security executives share some of
the secrets to their success and the resources they relied on to
get there.

*With insight from Dwight Williams, vice president of security
for DynCorp International LLC; Lorna Koppel, director of IT
security with Kohler Company; Jim Hutton, director of the
global security department of Procter & Gamble; Leslie
Lambert, CISO and vice president of IT for Sun Microsystems;
Bob Pappagianopoulos, CISO of Partners Healthcare System
Inc.; Miki Calero, CSO for the City of Columbus, Ohio; Jerry
Brennan, founder of Security Management Resources; and David
Burrill, former head of security for BAT Industries*

Learn to motivate and engage your staff so they will be
more likely to want to work with you to better security.

*By Karl Perman, manager of corporate security programs
for a large energy company*

If everyone in security acts as a leader, the security
program will achieve greater success and better alignment
with business goals.

*With insight from Joe Nelson, Security Executive Council
Emeritus Faculty in charge of the Security Leadership
Information Sharing Initiative; Radford Jones, an academic
specialist in the Michigan State University School of Criminal
Justice; Daniel Diermeier, professor of Managerial Economics
and Decision Sciences at the Kellogg Management School;*

Learn how to overhaul your security department following a drastic organizational change or due to a functional flaw with these lessons in reinventing security.

By Chris Berg, senior director of corporate security and safety for Symantec Corporation

PART 3 LOOKING FORWARD

Planning strategies for security leaders being asked to run corporate social responsibility (CSR) programs.

With insight from Francis D'Addario, former vice president of Partner and Asset Protection for Starbucks Coffee and Emeritus Faculty member of the Security Executive Council

Reflections on how security leaders have made recent advancements, and where they have hit a wall.

By Bob Hayes, former CSO of Georgia-Pacific and managing director of the Security Executive Council; and Kathleen Kotwica, PhD, executive vice president and chief knowledge strategist of the Security Executive Council

Begin to think about how to pass on your accumulated strategic security knowledge to your peers, staff, or successors with these ideas for a new kind of training program.

By Bob Hayes, former CSO of Georgia-Pacific and managing director of the Security Executive Council; and Kathleen Kotwica, PhD, executive vice president and chief knowledge strategist of the Security Executive Council

Boost the strategic thinking and planning skills of your direct reports by encouraging them to take on these 11 key strategic areas.

By Bob Hayes, former CSO of Georgia-Pacific and managing director of the Security Executive Council; and Kathleen Kotwica, PhD, executive vice president and chief knowledge strategist of the Security Executive Council

Strategies for preparing nimble, resourceful, and creative security solutions that match the speed of the new kinds of threats and risks security faces.

With insight from Francis D'Addario, former vice president of Partner and Asset Protection for Starbucks Coffee and Emeritus Faculty member of the Security Executive Council

Risk strategy guidelines for the ever-evolving and complex nature of business, and predictions for what security could be in the year 2020.

By Francis D'Addario, former vice president of Partner and Asset Protection for Starbucks Coffee and Emeritus Faculty member of the Security Executive Council; Bob Hayes, former CSO of Georgia-Pacific and managing director of the Security Executive Council; and Kathleen Kotwica, PhD, executive vice president and chief knowledge strategist of the Security Executive Council

Please note that the security practitioners who contributed to these articles may no longer be at the companies listed in the chapters.

INTRODUCTION

Over the past decade, the role of the security professional, from the beginning manager to the chief security officer, and the expectations that come with the position have been elevated to senior levels within the organization. These changes have been driven by a succession of events (acts of terrorism, increasingly frequent natural disasters, mass shootings, and global unrest). Organization changes and unique corporate cultures nearly eliminate the possibility of a singular way to accomplish a task. Having several strategy options available that can fit well within your existing organizational convention is a valuable resource. More than ever, the security industry is in desperate need of a new generation of leaders who are equipped to handle the challenges of not only today's security landscape, but more importantly, tomorrow's.

In 2013 The University of Phoenix sponsored a research project that examined enterprise security risks and workforce competencies.[1] The focus of the study, titled "Enterprise Security Risks and Workforce Competencies," was security talent development; the purpose was to identify the top risks the industry will face in the next five years and the skills that security professionals will need to demonstrate to protect tomorrow's enterprises. Security industry challenges of the aging work-force and the shortage of talent to replace current practitioners over the next two decades ranked high on the list.

Enterprise diversity, corporate cultures, and security challenges require every member of the security organization to be a leader to some degree. New and emerging issues, budget fluctuations, new product introductions, mergers and acquisitions (M&A), and the transition of baby boomer leaders into retirement provide numerous opportunities to lead if individuals are ready. Threats, threat response, and mitigation strategies are constantly evolving. The speed with which global events impact us all will increase significantly. Your ability to think and act with agility will

[1]University of Phoenix, "New Report Identifies Security Industry Risks and Necessary Workforce Skills," University of Phoenix news release, October 4, 2013, http://www.phoenix.edu/news/releases/2013/09/new-report-identifies-security-industry-risks-and-necessary-workforce-skills.html, accessed February 7, 2014.

be key. The bench strength of your team will also be critical, as multiple occurring global events will require a delegation of responsibilities within your organization to ensure that each issue is managed effectively. Preparing yourself and your team today for tomorrow's challenges is every senior leader's responsibility.

How do you, as a security executive or manager, stay current with these issues, familiarize yourself with the range of successful practices being implemented by your peers in other companies, and transfer this information to build a knowledgeable, skilled workforce the times now demand?

Security Leader Insights for Success is a collection of timeless leadership best practices featuring insights from some of the nation's most successful security practitioners.[2] This resource is a quick and effective way to bring staff and/or contractors up to speed on leadership issues. In the event that you are forced to make rapid, significant change within your business or organization, this resource can help guide transformational change. Instead of reinventing the wheel when faced with a new challenge, these proven practices and principles will allow you to execute with confidence knowing that your peers have done so with success.

Dave Komendat
Vice president and chief security officer of a Fortune 50 company

---

[2]Please note that the security practitioners who contributed to these articles may no longer be at the companies listed at the time this book is published.

PART 1

The Skills Needed for Successful Security Leadership

CHAPTER 1

The Art of Leadership

With insight from Dwight Williams, vice president of security for DynCorp International LLC; Lorna Koppel, director of IT security with Kohler Company; Jim Hutton, director of the global security department of Procter & Gamble; Leslie Lambert, CISO and vice president of IT for Sun Microsystems; Bob Pappagianopoulos, CISO of Partners Healthcare System Inc.; Miki Calero, CSO for the City of Columbus, Ohio; Jerry Brennan, founder of Security Management Resources; and David Burrill, former head of security for BAT Industries

In the headlines we read much more about leadership failures than leadership successes. The security professional aspiring to that coveted corporate executive position may find it daunting to watch the parade of fiascos and consequences the past several years have brought: Enron, HP, BAE, HealthSouth, Vivendi, Parmalat, and political disasters like the mishandling of Hurricane Katrina, Halliburton contracts, and Walter Reed. While there's much to be learned from these leadership breakdowns, do their lessons really apply to security leadership? If so, what can the aspiring security executive do to develop the skills that will help him or her avoid similar catastrophes once in the top position?

Getting the best answers to these questions means asking them of the right people—corporate security executives who've already faced the lions and become recognized, both in their organizations and the industry at large, as successful leaders. Several members and faculty of the Security Executive Council agreed to share some of the secrets to their success and the resources they relied on to get there.

1.1 WHAT IS GOOD SECURITY LEADERSHIP?

Jerry Brennan, founder of Security Management Resources, a global executive search firm dedicated to corporate security, emphasizes the importance of first recognizing the difference between management and executive leadership. "A leader is a visionary, someone who can drive strategy and who understands the levers of power in the corporation, and someone who can clearly articulate his or her vision. There's a lot of marketing involved in that. A manager has to think strategically as well, but there you're dealing with people leadership, results and personal leadership, effective delegation, rewarding performance, developing employees." Many executive positions today ask for a combination of leadership and management skills, says Brennan, but it's important for the security professional to clearly understand the differences between them.

Leadership is not about telling people where to go and what to do; it's about showing them the path you would like them to take and inspiring them to follow it. "The basis of leadership is having the characteristics that cause people to *want* to follow your lead—to listen, adapt and follow your example," says David Burrill, former head of security for BAT Industries (British American Tobacco), a major global insurance and tobacco conglomerate, and founder of Burrill Green, a management consulting firm for corporate security.

Security leadership at the executive level is in essence no different than executive leadership of any other business unit. "In the corporate world you need to be a business leader, period," said Dwight Williams, vice president of security for DynCorp International LLC, a multi-billion-dollar provider of specialized technical services to government agencies. "It's about the business at the end of the day."

While knowledge of the security field is an important factor of success, the ability to talk business at a level on par with other corporate executives is critical. Burrill explains, "The rest of the C-suite needs to look at the individual and say, 'That guy is like us. He has different technical competencies but we're comfortable with him, he'd fit in well, and he's bound to bring value to us which extends beyond the pure efficiency of his function, which happens to be security.' If the senior executive doesn't have that sort of profile he will always be looked upon as a corporate cop. He'll be there because he has to be, but nobody will discuss anything but security with him because they don't reckon he'll understand, and if he does, they don't reckon that he'll bring any thought leadership or value to any conversation in which he is involved. That's pretty damning."

If business skills are vital, what specific business knowledge, skills, and characteristics must the security professional develop to avoid being seen as the corporate cop?

1.2 WHAT KNOWLEDGE, SKILLS, AND CHARACTERISTICS DO YOU NEED?

1.2.1 Know the Culture

Success begins with knowing business culture in general and the culture of your business in particular. According to David Burrill, one of the most difficult challenges for security professionals coming out of the public sector is learning to understand how the private sector works. The gap between public- and private-sector processes is wide, but can be overcome by the attentive and open-minded professional.

Lorna Koppel, director of IT security with Kohler Company, says that learning the culture of the organization and where you fit into it is first priority for leading successfully in the context of the company. "Be highly observant and watch others around you at your level and higher. Pick up things they're successful at and avoid things that they're less successful at." Your leadership style should depend upon the culture and needs of the company, says Koppel.

Jim Hutton, director of the global security department of Procter & Gamble (P&G), agrees, adding that you also need to recognize and remedy any disconnects between your style and the organization's. "Understand that what you think you need to deliver may not in fact be what they need. What you're good at or best prepared for may not be the best fit for the new mission. Being willing to address the gap between your background and the mission is really important; you have to be confident enough to go out and learn new things."

1.2.2 Enable the Business

Leading security is your job, but you can't succeed at it unless you put the needs of the business first and then tailor security to those needs. "I tell my people that we start from yes, we don't start from no," says Hutton. "We may have to heavily caveat our yes sometimes, but it's a general rule. We make them mindful of the constraints, but we enable them. And then the 5 percent of the time I have to say no, absolutely no, they'll listen."

"You have to know the risk appetite of the company and how you can match your security program to that," said Leslie Lambert, CISO and vice president of IT for Sun Microsystems. Security is traditionally viewed as a naysayer, always telling the company what it can't do.

"But we should be learning to talk to business folks about what is possible instead of listing out all the limitations," Lambert says.

If your security stance doesn't resonate with the business, adds Kohler's Koppel, you can't expect business to change. You have to change your message. Corporate security may have legitimate and even critical concerns, but if they deal with them in a way that's counter to business goals, they'll fail.

1.2.3 Know Security

While business knowledge is the number-one priority for successful security leadership, an in-depth knowledge of security—specifically corporate security—is obviously also important. But that doesn't mean you have to be an experienced installer, says David Burrill. "You wouldn't expect a leader to be able to site CCTV or directly run a guard force or know how to break into a combination safe. But you would expect him or her to know that there is a range of activities for which there must be technical competencies, and to know that the people he's employing or outsourcing to have the adequate competencies," he explains.

Security acumen is critical because, according to P&G's Hutton, "your solutions are going to have to be well grounded and well crafted. Executives are getting more sophisticated in this space." If you're proposing a solution that's outdated or has proven ineffective at a similar organization, decision-making executives will recognize that and shoot you down.

1.2.4 Communicate Effectively

Communication is key to successful security leadership, both with other executives and with the security team below you.

"As security professionals in the corporate or IT side, we have to be strong in business language. If we can't present our issues in a business framework or in business lingo, (C-suite executives) are not going to understand what we're talking about and they're not going to understand why we care," says Koppel. And if that's the case, they're certainly not going to support your initiatives.

Effective communication with senior management must begin with the very first meeting, says Bob Pappagianopoulos, CISO of Partners

Healthcare System Inc. "Don't go to senior management the first time and ask for money. When you have your first meeting with the people with the purse strings, make sure it has nothing to do with asking for funds. Find out what floats their boat—economies of scale, efficiencies, fast fixing—and then focus your requests on something that would interest them."

The same rule applies to communication down the chain, with your security team. As soon as you're appointed to a leadership position, says Pappagianopoulos, "have a meeting with all the people in the room. Even if they're at different locations, you have to have a physical meeting and say 'Here are the guiding principles I tend to manage by,' so they know." If you're open about your style and expectations from the beginning, team members can begin adjusting to your leadership immediately.

Make yourself available in person or by phone or e-mail, and make sure your employees know they can contact you with any question. When they do contact you with a question or concern, listen carefully, take it seriously, and give them a helpful response. When you receive e-mails from employees, reply to them, addressing the sender by name. According to Miki Calero, chief security officer (CSO) for the City of Columbus, Ohio, you can't overestimate the impact of a personal touch. "People respond to you if you care about them," Calero says.

"I practice Management By Walking Around," says Dwight Williams of DynCorp. "It's important to be seen. It's important to let people know you're involved, you care, and there's a sense of urgency about what you're collectively doing. It's hard to do that if you're never in the office or you're never around your team."

Sun's Lambert says that she's recognized that her team performs better if she shares her thinking with them, explaining how she reached a given idea or conclusion. "If you can teach your staff to do what you would do, you don't have to micromanage anybody. And if your team doesn't 'get it,' maybe you're not showing them how you got there and what it's all about."

1.2.5 Build the Right Team

"There's a strong correlation between team chemistry and success," says Calero. "Without team chemistry, you will be thrown more often into micromanagement." When you as a security leader have the opportunity to create your team from the ground up, you're at an advantage. Don't rush to fill positions; take your time to find the right people. Recognize that you must choose based not only on experience, but on character, says Pappagianopoulos. Will they collaborate? Are they inquisitive and flexible? Will they listen and share their own observations? These are all important factors to consider.

If you're coming into a position where the security team already exists, you have a greater challenge. Calero says, "I dedicate a lot of time to understanding what each (of my existing team members) can do for me. Then I envision how each can meet a specific need, which can build on another's strengths, in all contexts. This is not a quick process; it has to have time. You have to know how to bring the most out of them."

1.2.6 Be Flexible

Jim Hutton believes that an inability to be flexible is a deal-breaker for successful security leadership. In a business environment where acquisitions and divestitures are in the headlines every day, the security leader has to be ready to move where the company takes him. "Have an intellectual curiosity on how to follow the business," he says. "Be mindful of fact that the job you take may become very different in a short period of time."

1.3 WHERE CAN YOU GET THOSE SKILLS?

A security professional interested in moving up to the executive level can leverage a number of resources to help him or her develop the skills of quality leadership. It's important to start this development process early. According to Security Management Resources' Jerry Brennan, "If the job is looking for an executive leader to drive strategy, they are not going to want somebody in training." They'll be looking for the executive confidence, communication, and vision during the interview process.

P&G's Hutton recommends that security professionals begin their leadership development two years before they hope to transition to an executive role. That gives them ample opportunity to take advantage of any training provided by or assisted by their current organization.

MBA programs, while longer and more expensive than some other training options, will pay dividends to the security manager looking to become the security executive. Other programs exist specifically to train security leaders in executive leadership skills, such Johns Hopkins University's Police Executive Leadership Program, the International Security Management Association's Leadership Programs in partnership with Georgetown University and Northwestern University's Kellogg School of Management, and the Wharton/ASIS Program for Security Executives. "The Security Executive Council is also a marvelous vehicle for learning," says David Burrill.

Individual courses on presentation skills and financial acumen are offered by many universities and business organizations as well, and internal training provides another valuable resource.

"Pick up a little reading," recommends Kohler's Koppel. "There are plenty of management books out there. Pick books that are written for a higher level than you're at. If you're a manager, pick up something at executive level, and pay attention to the language."

Burrill encourages aspiring leaders to find coaches or mentors who are already proven leaders in the field. "Some people don't like the title (coaching or mentoring) because they feel it implies they're deficient, which is nonsense. The people who have the most potential are the people who are most prepared to seek a coach or mentor. The weaker people tend not to, perhaps because they don't want to appear that they need help or they lack confidence in their own ability." In reality, says Burrill, working with a mentor is peer-to-peer, bouncing ideas around with someone who has had a similar experience.

While coaching is extremely useful, say Calero and Lambert, always remember to take your mentor's advice in the context of your own situation and not to discount your own instincts.

1.4 CAN LEADERSHIP BE LEARNED?

All the above resources exist to train individuals in the skills needed to achieve strong leadership, but successful leadership also relies upon certain traits and intrinsic personal qualities, such as vision and the ability to inspire and motivate. Can these be taught? Burrill contends that they cannot. "There is an issue of aptitude," he says. "With the right aptitude, people can learn. I believe leadership is natural to a person but can be improved with training. But I don't believe with training you can make a person who does not have leadership aptitude into a leader."

If you aren't sure if you have that aptitude, you could pay a fee to take what's called a psychometric test to determine if you have the characteristics that lend themselves to successful leadership. Or you could take a good hard look at yourself. Jim Hutton advises, "Candidates should look at what motivates them and what their experience has been. Do you have the skill set to be CSO for a $20 billion company? What do you bring to the table? What can you develop in yourself? Determine the right job for you; don't just apply to every job you see."

CHAPTER 2

Be the Great Motivator

By Karl Perman, manager of corporate security programs for a large energy company

There's a good deal of research out there that indicates that employees who are happy, engaged, and committed in their jobs are more productive and more loyal workers. There's also research that shows that higher employee satisfaction in a company often correlates with higher customer engagement, satisfaction, and brand loyalty.

A lot of us security practitioners may glance at statements like these and assume they're meant for the vice president's and the chief executive officer's (CEO) eyes only. That's their responsibility as the business leaders of the company and the crafters of the corporate culture, right?

Not really. Yes, it is their job on a company-wide level, but it's our job too. If we have staff, then engaging and motivating them is our job.

It's good for business. I think that everyone in a supervisory or management role in a company should view themselves as responsible for the well-being and success of that company, no matter where that person is located on the reporting chain. A strong bottom line is good news for all of us, and there's evidence that employee satisfaction contributes to a strong bottom line. The findings of a 2001 study published in *Personnel Psychology* journal, for instance, support the idea that employee satisfaction, behavior, and turnover can be good predictors of company profitability and customer satisfaction.[1]

It's good for security. I believe that you get more from a carrot than a stick. More than likely, if you're not motivating your employees, no one else is. They are not being as productive as they can, and they're not performing to their utmost potential. More motivated employees are more aware, more innovative, and more engaged, which means, in

[1]Daniel J. Koys, "The Effects of Employee Satisfaction, Organizational Citizenship Behavior, and Turnover on Organizational Effectiveness: A Unit-Level, Longitudinal Study," *Personnel Psychology*, 54, (2001): 101–114, doi: 10.1111/j.1744-6570.2001.tb00087.x.

our context, better security, business continuity, executive protection, or emergency management.

It's good for us. It's a lot easier to do your own job well when you're not surrounded by negative, apathetic, or disengaged co-workers and employees. If you can successfully motivate and engage your staff, they will be more likely to want to work with and for you.

2.1 IT'S NOT ALWAYS EASY

Motivating staff is easier in some atmospheres than in others. If a corporate culture of employee appreciation and engagement already exists in your company, chances are there are motivational tools built into the system. The top 10 on *Fortune*'s "100 Best Companies to Work For" list tend to have stellar benefits, great compensation, and unconventional frills for employees. But a lot of companies don't have that kind of baked-in positive culture, and some who used to have it have marginalized or abandoned it to focus on the bottom line in the economic recession.

Pay cuts and layoffs are demoralizing, particularly if they're done the wrong way. If your company is dealing with employees in such a way that it makes them feel they're being treated unfairly, their first inclination is probably to shift most of their on-the-clock effort from doing their job to looking for another one.

In these situations, you may feel that motivating your staff is an uphill battle. Not only do you have to counteract the effect of the overall apathy and anxiety permeating your company, but you have to put on your game face and be a little more optimistic yourself. Griping along with employees about the ills of management is not going to motivate anyone; you have to accentuate the positive and find ways to take care of your people.

Here are some things you can do to help motivate your employees whether you have the support of the corporate culture or not.

- Identify all the benefits the company offers, from tuition reimbursement to 401(k) matching contributions, and make sure your staff knows about them and recognizes the importance of taking advantage of them.

- Give your employees SMART (specific, measurable, attainable, realistic, and timely) goals. This will help them to feel a sense of accomplishment on a regular basis.
- Tell them when they're doing a good job.
- Don't underestimate the power of small gestures, like having an occasional casual dress code day.
- Make some sacrifices, like taking the team out to lunch even if you have to pay out of pocket.
- Break out of the ordinary. Have off-site team-building exercises when you can, or invite an outside speaker to speak at a team meeting, for example.

2.2 LEARN AS YOU GO

If you're not naturally charismatic or inspiring, that doesn't mean you can't do a good job of motivating your employees. This kind of skill can be learned. Do a self-analysis or get a coach or a peer group to help you assess your motivational skills and offer you methods for improvement. Read. There are a lot of books out there about the components of leadership and how to motivate people.

Think about how you can motivate your staff members and then take action. Be motivational. I believe you will find that it is well worth the effort.

CHAPTER 3

Becoming a Business Leader

With insight from Joe Nelson, Security Executive Council Emeritus Faculty in charge of the Security Leadership Information Sharing Initiative; Radford Jones, an academic specialist in the Michigan State University School of Criminal Justice; Daniel Diermeier, professor of Managerial Economics and Decision Sciences at the Kellogg Management School; Joseph Hannigan, the program's associate director of Executive Education at the Kellogg Management School; Tom Mahlik, chief of the Domain Management Section of the Federal Bureau of Investigation's (FBI) Directorate of Intelligence; and Dan Rattner, visiting scholar at the College of Professional Studies and College of Criminal Justice at Northeastern University

My company's prime objective is not to stay secure. Its objective is not to manage its own risks or maintain business continuity or protect its assets or detect network intruders. My company's objective is to

_____.

Most corporate senior management teams expect their security leaders to be able to easily fill in this blank. Many also expect their CSO or equivalent to take it a big step further by linking every one of the company's security-related initiatives with that objective. Even CEOs who have shown little direct interest in security are starting to follow this trend. It's all part of business' evolving understanding of what security leadership is and who should be practicing it.

3.1 THE ELEMENTS OF LEADERSHIP

In 2006, the Security Executive Council conducted a study that found that companies were increasingly hiring professionals with business backgrounds into their top security positions. These results followed a long trend: Historically, companies have predominantly hired security leaders with backgrounds and experience that speak to the most pressing issues of the day (see Figure 3.1).

In the 1950s and '60s, they looked for military veterans; in the late 1970s and early 1980s, many began to focus instead on a background in law enforcement. From the '80s through the mid-'90s, corporations

Figure 3.1 A historical timeline of the backgrounds from which security professionals have been hired.

began promoting security leaders from inside their own business who were familiar with their company's culture, internal processes, brand, and customers. At the same time, companies began reacting to international competition, quality initiatives, and technology by hiring managers with executive leadership skills, such as the ability to manage large budgets, negotiate, influence peers, coordinate external initiatives, lead staff, and communicate and present effectively. And with the advent and growing popularity of the Internet in the mid-1990s, many organizations began hiring IT professionals to head security programs company-wide.

The trend of hiring businesspeople as security leaders actually began in 2003 and 2004 when companies started looking for business skills, such as an ability to align security with the business and to add value through security functions, in response to extreme competition and pressure on Wall Street to maximize profit and minimize cost.

The problem with companies' tendency to hire security leaders with single, narrow skill sets is that when the risk picture changes and the pressing issue of the day fades into the background, these leaders have a harder time adapting to the new challenges. Instead, long-term success in security leadership comes through a blended skill set that includes major elements from each of the knowledge areas we've mentioned, as well as another: awareness of emerging issues. (See Figure 3.2.)

Many security professionals who haven't come from business backgrounds continue to struggle to acquire or hone the business alignment skills that are becoming more and more necessary in today's business climate.

3.2 AERODYNAMIC SECURITY

Globalization has made companies more complex, and the more complex an organization becomes, the more difficult the security leadership role has the potential to be. In addition, as our economy continues to

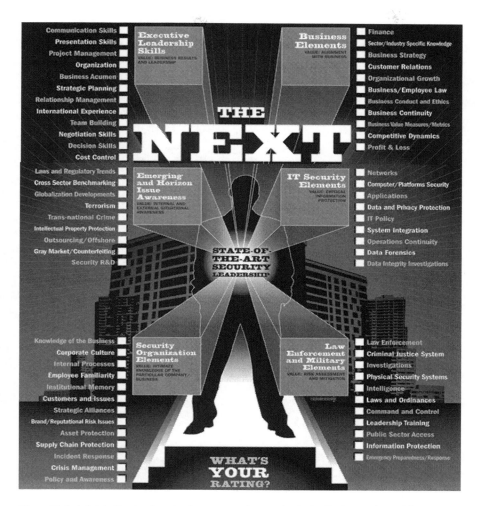

Figure 3.2 Included in the six elements of next generation security leadership is emerging and horizon issue awareness.

flounder, corporate boards and senior management are demanding more value and lower cost, and that means making sure that no dollar is wasted. Some are slashing budgets and staff just to stop the financial bleeding, but many are using the downturn as an opportunity to cut with surgical precision. These organizations are increasingly looking at "lean" principles and other management philosophies like Six Sigma and continuous process improvement to increase business efficiencies. They're eliminating waste—examining all elements of the business to determine which are critical to the success of the prime objective. Security isn't immune.

Knowing and working within the business strategy is the best way to succeed in such an environment, says Joe Nelson, Security Executive Council Emeritus Faculty in charge of the Security Leadership Information Sharing Initiative. "I call it aerodynamic security," Nelson says. "Just like an automobile, a high-performing organization has to be streamlined. It has to have very little to slow it down, and the proper security organization therefore takes on a shape that allows for optimization and less resistance. Residual risks have to be managed, so business leaders need executive security leaders who are dynamic, who understand the business environment and can navigate for the company the absolute optimum solution. This keeps the business moving at a rapid rate with the minimum number of encumbrances while at the same time optimizing the cost of security protection. That's a true skill."

Dan Rattner, visiting scholar at the College of Professional Studies and College of Criminal Justice at Northeastern University, has observed a gradual decline in senior security leaders without business acumen since 2001. "What we need to be able to do," he says, "is to continue to train people to be strong contributors at that level."

There are a number of programs of different types available to security leaders who want to work on these skills.

3.3 FOCUSED, ONLINE TRAINING

The SEC Live online seminar series was launched several years ago to give security practitioners in any location access to live seminars, presented by industry thought leaders, that deal with executive-level leadership concerns. Especially when budgets are tight and travel and conference funds are short, the online format is a good way to maintain and advance relevant skills.

Joe Nelson, who directs the program, says SEC Live seminars focus squarely on the business element skills that are so crucial today. Previous and upcoming seminars will cover topics like managing careers, business alignment, managing change, building on the company strategy, and developing core metrics. And the seminars are all based on tried-and-true thought leadership, built from the Security Executive Council's knowledge base and taught by industry veterans who have themselves led successful security programs at the executive level.

"We are very particular about the content and the value deliverable that we provide in SEC Live," says Nelson. "Participants not only walk away with deeper understanding of certain subject matter; they walk away with tools that they can use and apply directly."

3.4 EDUCATIONAL RESOURCES

Some security professionals strongly advocate that all executive-level leaders earn their MBA. This would certainly assist them in learning business element skills, but it isn't the only helpful option universities can offer. Some have degree programs and certifications specifically targeted toward security practitioners.

For 10 years, Michigan State University has been offering an online version of its on-campus master's degree program in security management. This graduate specialization deals with the business side of security, as well as administrative, legal, and management issues. Radford Jones, an academic specialist in the MSU School of Criminal Justice, says the university strives to present an advanced security management curriculum within a business context. "We want to develop leaders and managers who can provide to their executives a position paper that says what the risks are, what needs to be done, how it can be done cost effectively, and that shows some careful research into the expected results. We try to explain that security management is an integral part of the management of the business and you have to be part of that. Understand the culture of your organization. Understand the markets they're working in and the legal requirements of them."

MSU also offers three-course online certificates in various specializations, such as homeland security issues, threat assessment, public-private partnerships, and emergency planning, which are designed for individuals in any field who wish to enhance their understanding of these issues.

Jones adds, "We ask our students (many of whom are practitioners): What does the company website say? What is the business objective of the company? Your security objectives need to be lined up with that. Are you going in the same direction? Because if you're not, you're going to be the loser."

Like MSU, Northeastern University in Boston offers both an online master's program and certificate program. Northeastern's MS in criminal justice leadership is intended for both public- and private-sector practitioners, according to Dan Rattner. It focuses on issues of leadership, communication, integrity, and ethics, and Rattner believes it can also remove some of the barriers between the public and private sectors and enhance information-sharing.

The certificate program in security management, on the other hand, is designed specifically for mid- and senior-level security management professionals across industries who wish to learn about the connections between business functionality and the threat environment, as well as post-9/11 regulatory issues that play a role in this interaction.

"Absolute security is impossible when you are in a for-profit environment," says Rattner. "You have to accept some risk and transfer some risk, and you've got to make prudent decisions. If you go in always screaming that the sky is falling, you're going to lose credibility, and then you're done. What we need to do is continue to train and educate security practitioners to be good, smart, prudent businesspeople and understand that there is risk inherent in business. Otherwise you wouldn't be generating a profit."

3.5 CUSTOM PROGRAMS

Individual membership organizations and agencies in both the public and private sectors also offer training that is tailored for their members. The International Security Management Association (ISMA) developed a partnership with the Kellogg School of Management at Northwestern University to create the ISMA Senior Executive Leadership Program. Daniel Diermeier, professor of Managerial Economics and Decision Sciences at the Kellogg Graduate School, has been director of the program since its inception. "After 9/11 it became clear to everyone in the C-suite that security had become a very important corporate function. And that meant that CSOs were getting much more exposure to the C-suite and to board members, but many did not come from a business context and had difficulty interacting effectively with executives at the strategy level."

The Senior Executive Leadership program was designed to develop senior executives' leadership skills and to improve their ability to interact with their companies' senior management and corporate board. The program was initially for ISMA members only, but now it is also open to individuals who are recommended by a sponsoring ISMA member, according to Max Brenton, current president of ISMA.

The Federal Bureau of Investigation (FBI) has also partnered with Kellogg in a two-course executive development program that shows FBI executives, agents, and analysts how business concepts can be applied to their agency. Much of the FBI's executive education program concentrates on organizational change.

The program was born out of the shift the FBI experienced after 9/11, says Joseph Hannigan, the program's academic director and the associate director of Executive Education at Kellogg. "The FBI had always been consistently branded as 'the premier law enforcement organization.' After 9/11, they had to become a national security organization with a dual focus: continued excellence in law enforcement; and terrorism prevention and intelligence," he says. Considering that the agency already had a remarkably broad scope of responsibility, this shift added an entirely new level of complexity to an already intricate organization. The FBI began searching for training that would help its people—from the director to first-line supervisors—effectively lead and navigate the changes that were occurring in the FBI's mission. Recognizing that they could leverage the knowledge of the business world to meet this challenge, the FBI requested proposals from the country's preeminent business schools, and Kellogg won.

"We don't know intelligence," says Hannigan. "What we have is an understanding of how complex organizations work through dramatic changes. A lot of government agencies are coming to realize that they have a lot to learn from corporations and the business schools that educate the top corporate executives." The skills that help the program's students navigate the change from a singular focus on law enforcement to national security *and* law enforcement can be used to lead and manage future organizational shifts as well.

Tom Mahlik, chief of the Domain Management Section of the FBI's Directorate of Intelligence, has been through the program. He is leading a number of new intelligence program initiatives associated with the FBI's transformation and is impressed with the range and impact the training has had in helping to solve problems. "Kellogg has been able to blend a number of corporate best leadership practices into our culture and accomplish it in a way that inspires new thinking.

They understand the nuances and challenges we face as a public organization, and at the same time they're helping imbue the lessons learned from the C-suite of corporate America into the FBI—from leading change to managing in a crisis. The program has included a breakdown of business cases that introduce opposing perspectives, new ideas and alternative approaches to make FBI leaders better decision makers. What does 'good' change leadership look like? What internal and external communication networks need to be in place? What change implementation processes work?" All of this adds up to changed behavior on the part of each person who is playing a role in fulfilling the FBI's mission, says Mahlik.

3.6 BUSINESS WILL BECOME THE LANGUAGE OF DIALOGUE

The FBI's collaboration with the Kellogg School illuminates one more reason that business training is important for security professionals: It will enable more effective dialogue between the public and the private sector.

"Public-private partnership is such an important component both from the point of view of the [FBI] and the commercial sector," says Diermeier. "It gives the [FBI] an ally who can translate the need for anticipation and intelligence-gathering and quick response, and it gives the business a valuable asset to help manage the security function appropriately. The benefits of partnership are tremendous, but they get lost sometimes because you have two people speaking different languages and communicating different concerns. Having a CSO that can serve a business function on one side and an agent who understands how business operates on the other side makes it go so much more smoothly and increases the chances for success."

As the FBI increasingly reaches out to businesses to share information and protect the country's economic security, security leaders must do their part to learn the language that will unlock this dialogue.

3.7 EVERYONE IS A LEADER

When the FBI first launched the executive education program, it exclusively targeted high-level executives. But they quickly realized that the training needed to go further, according to Mahlik. "We needed to communicate this new way of thinking to all supervisors throughout the agency, because everyone is a leader in their own sphere of influence."

This philosophy applies in corporations as well. Security professionals who are several steps down the chain of command in their organization should not think they don't need to work on the skills discussed here. The security program will enjoy much more success if everyone acts as a leader in his or her own sphere of influence, walking in lockstep with the business and making the business' objective a personal mission.

How will you bring about change?

CHAPTER 4

Finding Time: Time Management Strategies for the Busy Security Leader

With insight from Derek Benz, CSO, Performance Materials and Technologies for Honeywell; and Bob Hayes, former CSO of Georgia-Pacific and managing director of the Security Executive Council

Security leaders don't have time. The best ones find time, or make time, for critical or strategic tasks that have a long-range payoff, but they often struggle to fit more into a workday that already stretches from dawn to dark. Finding ways to multiply efforts is a critical skill for living a sane and successful life as a security leader. Open-source documents and templates, effective networking and benchmarking, and staff development can all help you free up time, letting you focus on higher-level tasks or simply on getting home before your whole family is asleep. But these tools must be used carefully in order to be effective, or they will end up costing more time as you repair the damage and start over.

4.1 DON'T REINVENT THE WHEEL

One essential survival trick: Don't reinvent the wheel. Don't start a policy, a program, or a department from scratch when it isn't necessary.

Let's first make clear that sometimes it is necessary to build from the ground up. The only way to know whether that's the case is to consult or conduct a thorough risk assessment of the organization and to know or discover how the security program fits into the business. Examine security's mission and vision statements, or develop them if none exist. Consider or learn the organization's culture, goals, and business philosophy, and security's place within it. Be familiar with the existing security guidelines, policies, processes, and programs and understand how they're perceived by the organization; measure them to determine their effectiveness; demonstrate how they are or are not adding value to the business. Only with this kind of knowledge under your hat can you determine whether existing resources will provide the right foundation for the program or policy you need.

If policy or guidelines creation is the goal, then once you know what to look for, there are a number of places to look. While the corporate security profession lacks the standards and inter-organizational consistency of many other business functions, there is a surprising breadth of material out there that can serve as a foundation for your efforts, including policy templates, guidelines, and open-source presentations.

We've compiled a list—representative, but not comprehensive—of websites and organizations that offer downloadable policy templates, assessment materials, standards, and guidelines on a variety of security-related subjects, including information protection, crisis management and business continuity, risk assessment, overseas operations and travel, and physical security/premises protection. Visit https://www.securityexecutivecouncil.com/savetime for the complete list with links.

Resources like these can save you time, but it's important to use them with discretion. Only use open-source documents from sources you have good reason to trust, such as the ones in our list. Check the date to ensure the document hasn't been rendered obsolete by subsequent events. A crisis management–related template from before 2001, for instance, may not be the best source to start with. In addition, remember that a generic open-source document should not be plugged into any program without modification, and the changes security requires to fit it into the business may not be the only changes necessary.

"You need to go through a process both to determine what guidelines and templates you intend to use and to build them into your organization," says Bob Hayes, managing director of the Security Executive Council and former CSO at Georgia-Pacific. "HR and compliance and other stakeholders—they very seldom want to adopt artificial standards as a baseline. The general counsel doesn't tend to care for standards specifically because they entail a higher level of legal accountability.

"So there's a vetting process you have to go through to make sure you choose guidance that's going to work in our situation. And then you need to consider input from those other groups to help you customize the guidance or templates you choose. No product is going to work for everyone all the time. If the policy or guideline is going to touch a lot of employees, the collaborative portion of the process is even more important."

4.2 LEARN FROM THOSE WHO'VE BEEN THERE

Benchmarking among a few peer companies is another way to save time. Learning from others' experiences can help you avoid common missteps. It can also help you see how others are dealing with emerging threats, or why other programs have gained support for types of initiatives that have foundered in your company. It can help you see how other organizations are complying with security-related regulations, which is useful because most rules are limited to *what* to do, and don't include details on *how* to do it.

"There are several ways we can get benchmarks," says Derek Benz, CSO, Performance Materials and Technologies for Honeywell. "We can work with organizations like the Security Executive Council, or the Corporate Executive Board's Information Risk Leadership Council. We also have a network of friends and peers with whom, if we have any challenges, and they've already solved them, I'll set up some time and go out to their office to talk about the issue."

Participation in organizations like those Benz mentions can provide benchmarks that draw from a large pool of data to provide a broad and reliable picture of what other organizations are doing. This can help to target security's efforts, which is a time savings in itself.

While less formal benchmarking doesn't always amount to the discovery of best practices, it's certainly well worth the effort. It must be remembered that even within single industry segments, security functions and corporate goals are so unique from company to company that it may be hard to find peers whose programs would provide an appropriate comparison. Peer-to-peer benchmarking also requires faith that your peers will not disclose any details you provide them. "If we share any information it's highly sanitized," Benz continues, "but there's no doubt about it that a weakness in one company can also be a weakness in another. We're interconnected, and it behooves all of us to bring ourselves up a level as an industry. The rising tide lifts all boats."

4.3 BUILD A STAFF YOU CAN COUNT ON

Micromanagement is a stealthy but notorious time thief. If you feel like you have to have your hands in everything to ensure it's done right, you are wasting precious hours every day and you're limiting your ability to do your own job.

To fix this problem you need to know where it's coming from. A tendency to micromanage may sprout from a naturally controlling or anxious personality. This isn't the stuff of quality leadership. If you've done your best to surround yourself with talented people and you're still trying to do their jobs for them, the problem lies with you.

If, instead, you micromanage because you know from experience that when you leave tasks to your staff they are regularly done incompletely or incorrectly—the problem still lies with you. You may need to make some tough staffing and hiring decisions, or you may need to find a way to provide the existing staff more engagement, more opportunities to learn and grow.

Honeywell, says Benz, has created a career paths group to answer questions like "How do you retain people? What are the qualities of our critical people, and how can we make sure we have a career path for them here? How do we attract the best and the brightest?" The group is involved in recruiting and hiring as well as retention and promotion, and they work to ensure that quality staff and potential leaders are shown how much the organization values them.

When you as a security leader have the opportunity to create your team from the ground up, you're at an advantage. Don't rush to fill positions; take your time to find the right people. Consider more than certifications and experience during the hiring process; try to determine whether prospects have the character traits that would lead them to strong performance and that would fit well into your corporate culture and your team. These traits may include a willingness to collaborate, inquisitiveness, flexibility, or an observant nature.

If you're working with an existing security team rather than hiring, it may be beneficial to sit down and carefully examine the qualities and skills of each team member. Identify their greatest strengths and their weaknesses and see how you can shift their responsibilities, their placement, or their focus to maximize the former and minimize the latter.

Think about what training and development opportunities you can offer them to build their skills and confidence. This is a time-intensive process, but time spent on the front end can save you much more time over the long term, and it may also reduce turnover and increase the effectiveness of your function.

When the security leader can steal time from low-level or labor-intensive tasks, he or she can fill that time in dealing with strategic or horizon issues, things that can enhance protection efforts and give the business a competitive edge. A small time investment in staff development, benchmarking, and finding basic policy or guidelines documents can pay off in spades in the long run.

CHAPTER 5

Leading Up: Or, How to Build a Positive Relationship with Your Manager

With insight from Tim Baer, executive vice president, general counsel and corporate secretary for Target Corporation, and Frank Brod, corporate vice president of finance and administration for Microsoft, about what they expect from their direct security reports, Brad Brekke, Target's vice president of assets protection, and Mike Howard, general manager of Microsoft Global Security

How do you measure leadership success? Certainly, you can look down the chain and see whether your function and your team are accomplishing their objectives. You can usually tell if your staff is motivated and if they're eager to follow you. But strong leadership isn't just about how you relate to the people below you on the reporting ladder. It's also about how you relate to those above.

What your boss thinks of your performance and your function is an extremely important measure of your success as a security leader. It shows how well you're listening to the needs of the business as he or she articulates them. It also shows how well you're communicating your strategies to other business leaders. Both of these things provide a critical foundation for the success of the programs, policies, and people you deal with every day.

As the recession begins to ease, the greatest concerns of top executives are moving away from basic business survival issues back to innovation, profit growth, entrepreneurship, and building corporate reputation and customer loyalty. As the strategic direction and business needs of the company shift, the security leader must recognize the nature of the shift and be prepared to open a dialogue with his or her boss on how security can help the company achieve whatever new goals it has set. The only way this will happen is if a strong relationship is already in place and the boss already sees you, the security leader, as a business enabler whose objective is to help the organization succeed.

We recently interviewed two successful security leaders at very different companies, along with their bosses, to gain some insight into what that kind of relationship looks like and how it can be developed. Tim Baer, executive vice president, general counsel and corporate secretary for Target Corporation, and Frank Brod, corporate vice president of Finance and Administration for Microsoft, shared some similar thoughts about what they expect from their direct security reports, Brad Brekke (Target's vice president of Assets Protection) and Mike Howard (general manager of Microsoft Global Security).

5.1 BE A LEADER FIRST

Both the bosses we spoke to view security as one of many business functions, noting that while it is a unique discipline, its leaders should be held to the same standards as all other business leaders.

"I look for the same leadership skills in all of my senior managers or leaders," said Brod. "I look for the ability to articulate a clear strategy, to provide motivational leadership, mentoring and coaching of employees, to drive towards impeccable execution of their work tasks and to motivate their group and provide the right rewards, recognition and feedback to help them grow in those roles."

Tim Baer ties the work of all Target's leaders, including security, to corporate goals and strategy. "At Target, we expect our executives to be creative in their respective disciplines, connect their strategies to the broader organization, and to be confident and self-reliant," he says. "Target leaders must be ambassadors for the company's goals and objectives and think critically about how their teams contribute to our success. Of course, we expect every leader to be an expert in their own business and share that expertise across the organization. But characteristics inherent to successful leaders—like innovative thinking and integrity—are commonplace among Target executives."

These executives expect all their direct reports to be leaders first, then experts in their fields. They view security leaders as business leaders. One of the reasons the security leaders in these two organizations have been successful is that they have viewed themselves the same way.

Since being named VP of Assets Protection for Target in 2001, Brad Brekke and his team have effectively overseen a remarkable broadening of responsibilities for the company's security function. Assets Protection once dealt primarily with traditional retail security concerns, such as shrink and physical security, and while those concerns remain a priority along with employee and customer safety, they now also have a voice in all decisions pertaining to global risk mitigation. Target Assets Protection has led the development of programs that have earned the company wide regional and national acclaim: Target & BLUE, a public-private partnership initiative through which Target supports public safety efforts, and the Safe City program, which unites local law enforcement, businesses, and residents to reduce crime.

Mike Howard joined Microsoft as general manager of Global Security in 2002. Since then the company's employee population has more than doubled and Microsoft has increased its global footprint, adding locations in countries such as China and India. Howard has helped shift the perception of security away from guns and guards, building and communicating a strategy of global risk management, including internal intelligence and threat analysis. He has also leveraged new technology investments to generate revenue; Microsoft's global security operations centers (GSOCs), which provide central situational awareness and control over corporate locations worldwide, have become a showcase Microsoft technology. Security partners with sales and marketing to allow clients to tour the GSOCs to see what can be done with the technology available.

5.2 THE ROLE GOES BEYOND SECURITY

Mike Howard and Brad Brekke have both pushed the traditional limits of the security role, guiding their functions into the realms of value generation and reputation building. This is exactly the type of innovation their bosses expect of them.

Baer specifically emphasizes forward thinking and a tight pairing of security and corporate strategy as crucial elements of Brekke's success: "The role of the security leader is to be fully immersed in company strategies and key initiatives, understanding and anticipating existing and emerging risks and driving solutions to address them. The role of the security leader directly correlates with the success of strategic business initiatives."

Brod focuses on Howard's ability to build influence across organizational units through both his security responsibilities and non-security programs. "Mike has great influence across my staff, interrelating with leaders in other departments like real estate and procurement. He has outstanding educational skills; he reads and recommends management books for our people managers. Mike has also set up manager network rings, which bring together our people leaders throughout the organization in groups of 8 to 10. They meet every other month to network and to seek advice from peer managers on how to deal with shared issues."

Brod and Baer are certainly not alone in expecting more than traditional security from their security leaders. "The paradigm has been shifting in the last few years," said Howard. "If you're totally focused on security skill sets but you're not focused on risk mitigation or adding value to the business, as well as those core leadership skills and social skills that are necessary to help you navigate, you're not going to be as effective."

Research from the Security Executive Council backs up Howard's observation. The Council's 2007 report on Security Leadership Background Trends concluded that organizations were hiring more security leaders with backgrounds in business management and IT, whereas traditionally security leaders overwhelmingly came from backgrounds in law enforcement and military. Management was looking for a new type of security leader who could more easily add value through security and communicate risks in terms of business impact. The Council went on to develop the Next Generation Security Leader model, drawing on research and the expertise of Council faculty, which identified six areas of knowledge that the security leader of the future would need to master. These include business and executive leadership.

5.3 NUMBER OF INCIDENTS IS NOT THE ONLY METRIC

Many security leaders measure the success of their programs primarily by counting how many incidents have occurred and determining whether the number is dropping, growing, or staying the same. While that is a valuable metric, Brod and Baer agree that in their organizations, it's not the only way to gauge security's success. "We measure performance against company-based metrics such as incident reduction, financial performance and productivity as well as team member and guest survey results," said Baer.

"Microsoft believes in commitments and accountabilities," Brod stated. "So we have commitments for Mike and all our leaders. We expect impeccable compliance and execution. We also look at resource management. That is, how can we deploy the billions of dollars we have invested in facilities and 90,000 employees to provide security and access services in the most cost efficient and effective manner? We measure Mike also on his revenue influencing ability, and we measure the culture of respect and ethics. And in the end we're all looking to drive shareholder value."

Dropping the number of recorded incidents is great, but it's not enough. To be viewed as something other than a drain on the bottom line, security has to actually become something other than a drain on the bottom line, and they have to be able to show it. At Microsoft and Target, the security leaders are expected to uphold the corporate culture and create a rapport with internal and external customers, all while securing the organization's people and assets and building revenue opportunities.

5.4 PROACTIVE COMMUNICATION

After speaking with Brod and Baer, we discussed their thoughts with their security direct reports, Mike Howard and Brad Brekke. Neither was surprised by what his boss had to say. We asked them to share some of their secrets for staying so in synch with their boss's expectations. It all came down to maintaining formal, positive, and regular communication.

"Open communication is vital," said Brekke. "We keep everyone informed and remain realistic about risks and what we can do to effectively mitigate them for the company."

Howard elaborated on how he maintains his seat at the table, stating that when Brod came on board at Microsoft, Howard's first objective was to meet with him to give him the broad overview of what security was and what it wasn't. This included a tour of the GSOCs. "We immediately got him to our GSOCs to get him up to speed on the totality of our technology, how it interoperates with other aspects of our business, and how it ties into the corporation," said Howard. After that initial overview, Howard and Brod endeavored to meet regularly at what Howard calls "monthly synch-ups."

"From a tactical and strategic standpoint I can talk to him and keep him up to date on not just what we're doing but what our strategies are," Howard said. "When I have quarterly business reviews with my team, I'll have Frank come out and speak. I've also made sure to synch up with other senior execs in the company—especially those I know he's going to be dealing with—because I never want him blind-sided; I want to make sure everyone's on the same page."

Brekke also emphasized the importance of company-wide aware-ness. "It's really important to have a seat at the table to be the voice for your team and keep the business informed of emerging issues and risks. That said, since one person can't be everywhere at once, team engagement is essential to communicate security strategies and keep a finger on the pulse of emerging company issues and initiatives."

He added, "We work to build visibility into issues that impact the whole company—like safety or shortage—by leveraging dedicated communications resources and developing a culture where team members are cognizant of the risks. Eventually, people embrace their role and become ambassadors for an issue. For example, we've built a strong culture at Target where people understand the importance of safe stores and communities, which is critical to our success."

Because there is always residual risk, it's critical to ensure that all senior leaders remain vigilant even when no major incidents are occur-ring, Howard said. "Once a month we put out an executive intelligence summary to people like Frank and senior leaders in the corporation so even if we haven't had to mitigate an incident in a month or so, they stay informed of the fact that there's a lot of stuff going on in the world that could affect our business and business continuity. They know that security has a piece of those issues and we're tracking them."

5.5 ARE YOU LEADING UP?

While the insights provided by Microsoft and Target shed light on some valuable lessons for all security leaders, they don't necessarily reflect what your boss expects of you. However, that doesn't make it less important for you to know what your own boss expects. How can you excel if you don't know what you're shooting for?

Can you easily and clearly articulate your boss's expectations of you and your function? Can you say with confidence that your boss understands and appreciates the scope of what you do? Are you certain he or she feels well informed of the security strategy and future direc-tion? Have you been leading up the chain, or just down?

CHAPTER 6

Understanding Your Corporate Culture

With lessons learned from Mike Kalac, CISO and vice president of Information Security for Western Union

Before you implement new security measures of any type, you have to do a lot of checking. When you're launching physical security technology, such as a new surveillance system, you check hardware and software, your policies, and staffing requirements. When you're revamping an emergency response program, you check your communications and backup plans, and you check with law enforcement. And when you go live with new network security measures, you check all the connections and rules, and you check with your support desk to make certain they're ready for calls. But in any of these instances, do you think to check the potential impact on the corporate culture? Believe it or not, that may be the most important check you're forgetting.

Mike Kalac, CISO and vice president of Information Security for Western Union, learned the importance of the corporate culture check when Western Union decided to move its Information Security (IS) function out from under the Information Technology (IT) umbrella. Kalac saw the change as a great opportunity. He welcomed the chance to give IS a stronger business role in the company. He and his colleagues immediately began working on a two-year roadmap for IS based on the projected development of the organization, assets, and technology.

After careful planning, Kalac's team chose several new technologies and tools and updated company usage policies to reflect the new security focus. The new solutions would provide a more secure corporate network by, among other things, employing web filtering to block access to select external sites and to scan downloaded files, and loading a client on personal computers (PC) that enabled asset tracking, better patch management, and locking down risky applications. Kalac was satisfied these decisions would best meet the needs of the company, and IS began to announce the upcoming changes to employees. The response came much more quickly than he expected.

"When we began sending out communications to let employees know what we were doing and how it would impact how they worked, we immediately started getting feedback from employees saying, 'Why are you trying to stop me from doing my job?' and 'You can't just put everyone under lockdown,'" said Kalac. It's not unusual for IS to get complaints from employees about new security measures, so at first they assumed these responses were just a more vehement version of a normal staff reaction.

"When I met with the internal colleagues to talk about filtering," Kalac remembered, "we were discussing what employees would be allowed to run on their PCs, and I made the statement that we won't support programs like iTunes. Feedback based on that comment was that as a company, 'We encourage our employees to use iTunes and also other internet sites used to balance their personal and work life.'" The team explained that in many cases employees are working between 10 and 15 hours per day, so they felt it was important to allow employees the benefit of doing some of their personal business, like banking, and enjoy some minor luxuries, like listening to their own music, while at the office. Also, the company was trying to reach out to a new generation of potential customers by advertising on social networking sites like Facebook and Myspace, so they would need to know if IS planned to block those sites as well.

Kalac left the meeting knowing that IS's new roadmap had done more than irritate a few vocal employees. "I discovered that when we started sending out communications on our plan, we were unwittingly playing with the existing corporate culture. Here we were in the security space stressing the importance of protecting the company from existing and new threats, and meanwhile the company culture was driving the work-life balance aspect and the need to access non-traditional, non-business websites. At the time I didn't realize that our actions would impact the corporate culture as much as they did." IS had always seen the corporation as security-minded, interested above all in information protection for customers both internal and external. Internal colleagues saw it as a business that wanted to show clients and employees that it was keeping stride with the times and technology and allowed some flexibility to employees who worked hard, long hours for the company. Western Union has a defined corporate culture, however managing security within a company that is doing business in over 200 countries requires a constant finger on the pulse of the company culture versus the security initiatives. "Knowing that security and culture of the company are not static, your must continually re-evaluate your impact on the company," Kalac states.

Kalac confirmed this discovery over and over as he met with other business unit leaders across the organization to talk about IS's new plan. His team considered each group's concerns and priorities, and then adjusted the IS approach to network security where the risk/benefits balance allowed it. One way they shifted their strategy, for instance, was to change their approach to site blocking. While some external sites must remain blocked, others that are important to various business units' cultural and business concerns are instead prefaced by coaching pages—pages that warn users that they may be entering risky sites.

Kalac believes the best way to gauge the cultural impact of a security change is to increase positive communication with colleagues and business leaders across the organization. "An information security leader should be concerned about reaching out to others in the organization to find out what the corporate culture wants to be and how to drive that culture," said Kalac. "This is something information security has to think about before it deploys a plan to secure the company."

CHAPTER 7

Rebuilding Influence after Corporate Restructuring

By Bob Hayes, former CSO of Georgia-Pacific and managing director of the Security Executive Council; and Kathleen Kotwica, PhD, executive vice president and chief knowledge strategist of the Security Executive Council

Company reorganizations are a fact of business that may have grown more frequent as our economy has changed in recent years. If your organization is going through one, or you believe there may be cause for changes in its governance and reporting structures, it is critical for you to think about the impact these changes may have on security's influence.

Will there be any personnel changes at the senior management level? If previously supportive people leave, all of the ground you covered and trust you earned while gaining support for your program may be walking out the door. Hopefully, you already have a metrics program in place so you can show new senior management an objective view of your program goals and accomplishments. Remember, brief and to-the-point presentations are crucial for this audience.

If you will be reporting to a new boss, there are several questions you should ask yourself. Have you taken steps to educate him or her about your program, the value it brings, and the results you have achieved? Are you able to effectively and quickly communicate the services the organization finds valuable, including the view from your boss' peers? Can you clearly articulate who the primary customers are of each security service? Can you demonstrate how each area of the company (audit, sales, comptroller, marketing, research and development [R&D], etc.) utilizes security? Can you demonstrate the cost, head count, and results of each program/service?

Get yourself to the place where you can answer "yes" to all of these questions. Then, after doing that, discuss with your new boss what he or she feels should be changed or modified. Consider reinventing or restructuring your security program in a manner that (re)appeals to senior management and (re)establishes it as a crucial partner within the organization.

How well have you been aligning your programs with corporate-level goals? Do you know how ready your organization is for your security programs? Do they look at them as reducing risk in well-defined areas (e.g., workplace violence or investigations)? Do they view security as a true business partner? Knowing how senior management views security will help you define your programs to meet their current expectations. You can't expect your programs to be accepted (or continually accepted) because they may have worked in the past. You must keep up with the ongoing transformations of the business.

You must also take a hard look at where you are as a security leader. Have you settled into a "maintenance" stance? While it is clear many security departments are currently understaffed and are working with a meager budget, consider the next stage you want to achieve. Try to find a way to keep existing programs well maintained while you build up your capacity to identify and manage emerging issues. If your department is thought of as simply a cost center, when the inevitable business shifts loom, you will surely be in the line of fire.

When corporate restructuring is on the table, take the time to think through your situation and the organizational structure. Then, plan strategies that will eventually get you back to the position of a valued, revenue-enhancing partner of senior management. And look at this as an opportunity to improve your function, build its influence, align it with business goals, and better reduce risk.

CHAPTER 8

Managing Expectations

With insight from John McClurg, vice president and chief security officer at Dell; and Bob Hayes, former CSO of Georgia-Pacific and managing director of the Security Executive Council

Problem identified and communicated, plan created, funds provided, problem resolved. This is the lifecycle senior business leaders often expect—and prefer—organizational challenges to have. It's the way decisions are made and issues addressed for many functions of the business.

Unfortunately, this naturally leads senior management to expect a similar lifecycle of security-related challenges: 1) Security apprises management of threats and vulnerabilities; 2) Management allocates funds to address them; 3) Problem solved.

However, it's rare that you can honestly say "problem solved" in security. Every little shift of the business, every new program or policy in a single department, every new piece of hardware and software installed, every external change to the market, global politics, even the weather—every one of these has the potential to introduce new threats and vulnerabilities into the organization's risk environment, sending the security leader back to the C-suite to say, "It's changed. We need more."

At the same time, management's baseline awareness of many security-related issues is high, due in part to a 24-hour media machine and an increased focus on risk brought on by the economic recession and other factors. "Management understanding is creating a new era in leadership expectation," said Bob Hayes, managing director of the Security Executive Council, in the final session of the Council's first Next Generation Security Leader (NGSL) executive development program.

Engaged management knows about many of the threats to business and expects security leaders to efficiently and cost-effectively manage the risks they face, and that's a good thing.

However, security leaders must take special care in this environment to communicate the inherent limitations of their craft. If they don't, those high expectations could turn into unrealistic mandates.

Even the most respected, successful and experienced security leaders must work to manage the expectations of senior management. John McClurg, VP and CSO at Dell, spoke briefly about this challenge during the NGSL final session and shared more in an interview afterward. McClurg has led successful security and risk functions at Honeywell International and Lucent Technologies, and he is a co-chair of the U.S. Overseas Security Advisory Council. Well-known and well-respected in security and business circles, he has found himself appreciating anew the impossibility of 100% protection.

"In recent years I've been humbled by the new vision and understanding I have of the incredible prowess and discipline of the adversaries," he said. "Notwithstanding our best efforts and our communication with leadership as to the nature of threats and vulnerabilities, it's not a question of 'if' but 'when' we're compromised.

"This is exacting of us more attention to the way we message what we need and what that expenditure can be used to produce in the near term. It also requires a clear, honest declaration of the prowess and ingenuity of the adversaries," McClurg continued.

It's an interesting challenge to say the least: to strike a balance in communication that inspires confidence in security's ability while clearly laying out the limitations of that ability; that avoids using fear to influence support while ever reminding management not to get too comfortable about their security. How does one strike that balance?

According to McClurg, "Whatever mechanisms you use to brief management on the threats you see emerging—bolster those conduits. So it may be that you increase the frequency of briefings because of the speed at which the change is occurring. What may have been adequate as an annual brief may now require quarterly or semi-annual updates. Even the tone of the message may need to be adjusted. The common phrase you hear is that we should under-promise and over-deliver. But we even need to be careful of what we think 'under-promise' means."

In communication and in action, security must focus not only on mitigating risk, he continued, but "on how resiliently we've positioned ourselves to move and adjust, and how well we have thought through the way we architect our structures and enclaved our most critical assets, to decrease the likelihood that the inevitable compromise will result in unacceptable loss.

"A conservative position one might adopt," says McClurg, "is to try to focus on the actuality while poised agilely to respond to the theoretical possibilities for which you haven't expended funds. In that environment particularly you may have to request funds more frequently, but hopefully if you explain that strategy, [management] will understand that you're trying to control spend in an environment in which you could easily spend endlessly."

CHAPTER 9

Running Security Like a Business

With insight from Francis D'Addario, former vice president of Partner and Asset Protection for Starbucks Coffee and Emeritus Faculty member of the Security Executive Council; and Kathleen Kotwica, PhD, executive vice president and chief knowledge strategist of the Security Executive Council

The next generation of security leaders will be challenged in ways previous generations have not. They will be asked to manage and monitor more risks and to identify and address new risks, including those created by drastic shifts in business operation and philosophy. They will have to do this more quickly, with fewer resources in many cases, and they will be expected to think and strategize at a board of directors' level.

· The security leader who prioritizes alignment will have built a strong foundation from which to meet the coming challenges of risk management. However, alignment is sometimes a significant challenge. It often requires current and rising security leaders to run security like a business, which includes knowing your business and its level of readiness for your strategies; communicating with and influencing internal customers; demonstrating how and where security resources are being used; and adding value to the organization.

First, if the security function hopes to align itself with the business' needs and goals, the organization, the security leader, and the security programs must all share the same level of "readiness." For example, the leader may be extremely mature, with years of experience and a long list of successes at other organizations, but if the organization is not ready for visionary security leadership—or not interested in it—then the leader may have to adjust in order to meet the company's needs. Or if the organization is prepared to shift from a compliance-focused security strategy to a proactive, growth-focused strategy, but the existing security programs are all built and measured around compliance concerns, a major shift in programs will be in order to match the readiness level of the organization.

A company's readiness may be impacted by many factors, including budget, senior leadership, and culture. To align with the readiness level of their organizations, security leaders must understand their own leadership maturity as well as the company's risk appetite, management's awareness level, and the drivers of security programs.

Running security like a business also requires communication and influence. A research report released by the Security Executive Council, *The Nine Practices of the Successful Security Leader*, identified commonalities between many highly successful individuals in their Tier 1 Security Leader community. (The report is available for purchase at https://store.elsevier.com/product.jsp?isbn=9780124116498.) "The findings in this report show that much of success revolves around communication and receptiveness," says Kathleen Kotwica, EVP and chief knowledge strategist for the Security Executive Council. "Each of our findings reflects how security or the security leader is perceived by other business leaders, management and employees based on how the security leader presents risk and, to a great extent, him- or herself."

In many organizations, security can also enhance alignment by helping improve the bottom line, either by reducing loss or building profit. In a business sense, risk management is not only about transferring or mitigating potentially negative risk; it is about identifying risk that may provide opportunities for growth or profit. While security has traditionally been expected to focus on mitigation, the global economic recession has caused many businesses to push all organizational functions—security included—to identify ways in which they can add value.

To align, therefore, security must extend beyond consequence protection. In order to enable this shift, security leaders will need to show a certain level of business acumen. They will need to be able to find the money by identifying opportunities in existing programs as well as potential value-adding partnerships with other functions. "The ability to promote transaction integrity—asset transfers, data, hiring, purchasing, sales and supply chain—through anomaly detection and mitigation will optimally pay for compliance programming and optimize the business," explains Francis D'Addario, former vice president of Partner and Asset Protection for Starbucks Coffee and Emeritus Faculty member of the Security Executive Council. D'Addario has a solid record of business-focused security success. "Injury, loss reduction, and revenue enhancement often yield more than 250% ROI with capable protection investment," he says.

CHAPTER *10*

Becoming a Next Generation Security Leader

By Bob Hayes, former CSO of Georgia-Pacific and managing director of the Security Executive Council; and Kathleen Kotwica, PhD, executive vice president and chief knowledge strategist of the Security Executive Council

No single skill set or attribute guarantees security leadership success. There are simply too many variables among industries, organizations, management, and security leaders for that.

The Security Executive Council's research report, *Nine Practices of the Successful Security Leader*, highlights commonalities identified between security leaders who are widely recognized as successful, both internally and externally. But while some of these nine practices—including conversing in business risk terminology and having a walk-and-talk management style—are the results of hard work, experience, and skill, other important factors, like having top-level support from day one, may be a matter of being in the right place at the right time.

Nine Practices of the Successful Security Leader was created from a series of in-depth practitioner interviews with security executives about their top organizational risks, business alignment and drivers, internal influence issues, and senior management's view of security. The resulting qualitative analysis uncovered nine practices that the interviewees with highly successful, internally recognized security programs had in common:

1. The creation of a robust internal awareness program for the security department, including formal marketing and communication initiatives
2. Ensuring that senior management is made aware of what security is and does
3. Walk-and-talk methodology—regularly talking to senior business leaders about their issues and how security can help
4. Conversing in business risk terminology, not "security"
5. Understanding the corporate culture and adapting to it
6. Winning respect by refusing to exploit fear, uncertainty, and doubt
7. Basing the security program goals on the company's business goals

8. Having top-level support from day one
9. Portraying security as a bridging facilitator or coordinator across all functions

Even if a practitioner focuses on achieving the nine practices that are under his or her control, they may not have the same results as they did for the security leaders discussed in the report. The acumen, personality, and priorities of the leader will impact how the practices are carried out and received by others in the organization. Likewise, the organization's view of security and the maturity of the security program can either nurture or stymie some of the nine practices. If management sees nothing more in security than incident response and physical access control, for example, then making them aware of what security is and does is crucial, but extremely challenging. Again, skill and aptitude are crucial, but success also depends on being in the right place at the right time.

Security leaders who aspire to become what we like to call Next Generation Security Leaders—future-oriented professionals who work across many domains, run programs that are aligned with their businesses, and are influencers in their organizations—should focus both on improving their aptitude and positioning themselves to be in the right place at the right time.

10.1 ASSESS TO FIND THE BEST EXECUTIVE DEVELOPMENT RESOURCES

Education comes in many forms, and not all of it is good or worthwhile. To determine what types of learning opportunities to pursue, security practitioners should first candidly assess themselves and their organizations in light of research like the *Nine Practices* report, peer feedback, and industry benchmarks.

They can review or perform organizational risk assessments to refresh their perspective on the risks and opportunities security can or should address. They should also review the organization's goals and evaluate whether security is helping to meet them. Then, a personal leadership assessment is in order to help the practitioner see the gaps in his or her skill sets and decide whether addressing them could help enhance security for the organization. Through this process, a security leader can best identify the educational gaps he or she most needs to address. The next step is figuring out how and where to bridge them.

10.1.1 Mentorship

Developing a mentorship with a more senior or retired security leader you respect and would want to emulate—preferably from within the same organization or industry—may be the best way to learn. Mentorship is more than shadowing or meeting for lunch now and again. It's a long-term relationship that entails sharing detailed knowledge and experience. Mentors can also enhance networking for their mentees.

The biggest problem with mentorship is a dearth of mentors. Truly innovative, visionary, business-focused security leaders are rare, and where they exist, it's unlikely they have the time to do much mentoring.

10.1.2 Educational Offerings

Again, a series of candid assessments should help point you towards education that would be relevant and helpful in your situation. Security-specific or industry-specific seminars offered by trade associations may be good sources for learning on certain security-specific topics. Business schools and industry-supported business programs may be more helpful for general business administration.

However, the Security Executive Council has found that while industry business programs help security leaders understand business practices and speak the business language, they fail to marry business processes with the job of risk mitigation. The Council is building a knowledge transfer program that addresses these concerns by including input from business professors, security industry veterans, and current practitioners—many of whom exemplify the nine practices listed earlier in this chapter. It has pinpointed 11 things that senior security leaders want to see in their staff and used these to guide the curriculum.[1]

Once you've begun building your aptitude, it's necessary for you to find an organization in which you'll be able to use it to the utmost.

---

[1] In conjunction with the University of South Carolina's Moore School of Business, the Security Executive Council is offering a six-month virtual long-distance executive development course. All available curriculum topics are established "proven practices" that every Next Generation Security Leader should have knowledge of. For information or to register, visit https://wwwhttps://www.securityexecutivecouncil.com/secstore/index.php?main_page=product_info&cPath=77_105&products_id=408securityexecutivecouncil.com/.

10.2 FINDING A JOB THAT ENABLES NEXT GENERATION LEADERSHIP

Putting oneself in the right place at the right time is a matter of effective career management. If Next Generation Security Leadership is your goal, every step of your career management strategy should be engineered to advance your journey toward it. This includes recognizing the organizational factors that play a role in achieving Next Generation–level success and building the job search, interview process, and decision making around those factors.

Some of the commonalities found in our research for *Nine Practices of the Successful Security Leader* may indicate how an organization or a security program can enable its security leader to excel. Consider what the following practices say about a prospective new employer and its existing security program.

- **The creation of a robust internal awareness program.** This is not employee risk awareness training; it is a formal marketing program that builds internal awareness of the security function and raises the understanding of what security does and the value it imparts to the organization. Program maturity is a significant factor here, as is corporate culture. It may be difficult or impossible to implement this practice if the existing security program is very small; if it is under-funded or under-appreciated; if it is recovering from major negative events that require all of the program's resources and time; or if the program's mission, vision, and goals are unclear even to the security function. These are things to look out for.
- **Ensuring that senior management is made aware of what security is and does.** Like building internal awareness, this practice's success depends on culture and maturity, and also on reporting structure and the perspective of upper management. Security Leadership Research Institute findings show that the reporting level of the security leader is a major factor in success and influence. It doesn't matter which function security reports through as much as how many levels away from the senior-most operating executive the security leader is. If senior leadership will not be accessible or does not appear willing or ready to listen to security, this should inform career decisions about the organization.
- **Understanding the corporate culture and adapting to it.** Is the culture something you can adapt to? If it runs counter to your principles or

your leadership style, consider truthfully whether you will be willing or able to adapt.

- **Having top-level support from day one.** This is arguably the most important predictor of success. Is the senior-most business leader a driver of or an inhibitor to security improvement? Does he or she buy into the value security can bring to the organization and hope to maximize that? Will he or she provide resources and authority to enhance the program and its value creation?

In his book *From One Winning Career to the Next*, J. David Quilter outlines a number of considerations for security leaders who are plotting out their next career steps. Many of the checklists and questions he provides to career seekers can help a prospective Next Generation Security Leader determine whether an organization is a fit for the practices above, as well as other factors of success.

Here are a few of the questions he recommends the job seeker think about during the interview process:

- Has the organization spelled out the responsibilities and accountabilities of the new security leader?
- Have there been numerous mergers or turnovers in key personnel? Have departmental and executive roles been sorted out in the aftermath of changes?
- What important security issues has the company faced within the last five years? How have they been resolved?
- Is there a well-established security function in place or is this a start-up?
- Is it clear to you what this company needs from you, and the timeframe in which they expect you to deliver on goals and objectives?
- Are existing security team members and others interested in personal and professional growth?
- Are members of the executive team participating in your interview? Can any of them discuss security with the same enthusiasm as they might speak of sales, marketing, finances, or operations? If not, what priority do you think they will they put on security in practice?
- Will you report to a C-suite executive and have access to the chair and CEO?
- How is the morale of operational managers?
- What about teamwork within departments? Are departments collaborative between each other?

- Are your questions answered honestly and without undue defensiveness?
- Do top executives trust others to lead within their departments, or do they merely want you to manage?
- Is the security organization fully integrated into the company?
- Does the corporation you are thinking of joining spell out its values? If so, how have they become part of the daily operation of the company? Are there ways in which the company evaluates itself behaviorally on specific criteria?

Quilter recommends that security leaders learn as much as possible about those to whom they will report through searches of publicly available information and other resources. They should speak with employees not in the presence of their interviewers and attempt to see how the company treats employees and security issues on a day-to-day basis.

Next Generation Security Leadership is a long-range goal for most. Developing the knowledge and skill sets it requires while carefully managing career moves—these are complex and challenging tasks, but they are worth the effort, and their results are worth the wait.

PART 2

Building Your Toolkit

CHAPTER 11

Developing Meaningful Security Metrics

With insight from Greg Niehaus, professor in the Darla School of Business, University of South Carolina; George Campbell, former Fidelity CSO and Security Executive Council Emeritus Faculty; and Dave Komendat, vice president and CSO at a Fortune 50 company

If security continues to mature as a business function, senior management will be increasingly likely to ask for a set of metrics to measure its performance, something that is already demanded of most other functions of business. Security leaders should be prepared to deliver meaningful metrics that are useful both for informing management and for improving security effectiveness.

The second session of the Security Executive Council's Next Generation Security Leader (NGSL) program explored the development and communication of meaningful metrics. The session and the online conversation that followed presented a number of questions security leaders should ask as they seek to identify and convey appropriate security metrics.

11.1 ARE YOUR METRICS TIED TO BUSINESS GOALS?

"Metrics should help us make better decisions," said Dr. Greg Niehaus, professor in the Darla Moore School of Business, University of South Carolina. "A good decision is one that furthers the organization's goals. Metrics should ultimately tie back to organizational objectives. Creating value is an important goal for most companies, so metrics should address that." The most likely indicator of security value is its impact on expected cash flow, so security metrics should be tied to that, Niehaus continued.

George Campbell, Security Executive Council Emeritus Faculty and author of *Measures and Metrics in Corporate Security*, agreed. "Security metrics are all about how you manage and define the value of security services," he says, adding that the importance of communicating this value is amplified by the fact that good security is often imperceptible to the entities being secured.

11.2 DO ANY OF YOUR METRICS SHOW VALUE BY RELIABLY MEASURING AVOIDED COSTS?

This question is closely related to the one above. Because security's value is often associated with what doesn't happen, it's important to estimate the cost avoided by mitigating events. One method of estimating these costs is examining the impacts of previous events on other organizations in your industry.

There are other ways as well. For example, a metric could be developed for background screening services by incorporating historical data and law enforcement statistics. Dave Komendat, VP and CSO at a Fortune 50 company, has done just that. "Certain offenses discovered in our screening process will bar applicants from being hired," he explains. "We know how many applicants are rejected each year on this basis and for what offenses. And we know the rates of recidivism for those offenses. So, if we reject 200 people a year because they have a theft background, we know from recidivism rates that if we'd hired those people, statistically speaking, 55% or 105 of them would potentially steal within a three-year period. We also know from statistics what the average cost of that theft would be in terms of lost assets, investigative costs, etc. So this allows us to demonstrate the range of cost avoidance we create on the program."

11.3 DO YOU COLLECT BOTH FORWARD-LOOKING AND BACKWARD-LOOKING METRICS?

Some metrics look ahead to facilitate decision making, and others look backward to assess performance, said Niehaus, and these two types of metrics are interrelated and equally important. For example, he said, "If you're going to invest in a system to reduce fraud, you'd like to know how much fraud to expect in years coming if you continue as is. In addition, you'd want to know how an investment in a new system would reduce frequency or severity of fraud. To build these two metrics, you have to look back at past data on fraud in order to forecast the expected frequency in the future. Forward and backward are related." Both types of metrics are required in order to most effectively inform decision making.

11.4 DO METRICS MEASURE DIRECT AND INDIRECT IMPACTS?

If a metric deals with the results of a recent or projected negative event, does it consider both direct and indirect impacts? Direct losses of a crisis may include lost wages, healthcare and response costs, and the cost of lost sales or services during downtime. But indirect losses such as reputational damage can increase the cost of a crisis by millions of dollars.

11.5 ARE YOU CREATING METRICS IN A VACUUM OR SOLICITING THE HELP OF OTHER FUNCTIONS?

An enterprise risk management approach is as applicable to metrics development as it is to risk mitigation. Discussing metrics with the leaders of other business functions can give you ideas about what to measure and where value can be found. It can also give you access to more data. Your legal or corporate insurance department, for example, could provide very useful assistance in measuring and communicating the cost of negative events. And, once metrics are created, they should be shared throughout the enterprise risk management (ERM) structure.

11.6 DO YOUR METRICS TELL A STORY?

George Campbell is fond of pointing out that there is a big difference between counting and measuring. "The data you need is out there. It's all over the place," he said during the NGSL session. "How are you using it to tell the value story? Do a current-state assessment of the data you have. Are you just counting things, or do the metrics you're using actually enable learning? Activity reports, incident reports, lists—they're not working for you until you put them in learning mode. What are they telling you about results? What do the incidents say about root causes? Do they measure results against employee action? Do they provide information about business value of security investment?"

"We learned early on the importance of understanding how to assimilate the data inputs and aggregate them into multiple data points to tell a story about productivity, quality, cost avoidance and risk mitigation," adds Komendat. "What types of information would be meaningful in a 30-minute presentation to the CEO and his leadership team? You have to know that."

If the metrics you're using are limited, if they don't tell a story, or if you don't use metrics at all, now is the time to ask these questions. "We live in times of scarce resources," said Campbell, "and this means somebody's measurements are going to be imposed on us. Do you want those measurements to come from you or from someone who knows nothing about security?"

CHAPTER 12

Setting Realistic Goals That Align with Business Interests

By Marleah Blades, former senior editor of the Security Executive Council

We see it a lot in the movies. A nation or a people is living under oppressive, tyrannical rule. They are cheated, impoverished, broken, and resigned to their lot in this life. Suddenly, a hero from outside enters and instantly grasps the injustice of the situation. He (it is nearly always a he) gives an impassioned speech, demanding they stand up and fight for their rights or their freedom.

Usually this movie ends with a war of epic proportions, in which the people overthrow the tyrants and the hero is memorialized for all eternity. But sometimes, before the final victory, we get a glimpse of an alternate universe—one that may be closer to reality. Every now and then, the hero gives his speech, and the people, invigorated, agree to fight, but they are quickly and soundly defeated. When this happens, they usually blame the hero. "Why did you drive us to this?" "We aren't fighting people." "Look at the damage you've caused!"

Now think of this in terms of a security program. You are the incoming director of corporate security. You walk in and see all manner of problems—evident risks unaddressed, policy gaps, inappropriate handling of events, lack of employee and management awareness, and a general malaise surrounding security. These are your oppressed people.

So you work feverishly to develop an amazing new security plan. You set your strategic direction and mission and you build from there, conducting a thorough risk assessment and lining up every type of mitigation program that the current system lacks. You consider industry-specific concerns and talk with peers and colleagues and integrate their experience-driven recommendations. You research technology and prepare to propose new applications. In short, you do everything right. When you're finished, you sit back and bask in the gleam of the best plan you could imagine.

And then you take it in to present to management.

Scenario 1: They love it. They agree to give you *carte blanche.* You implement every proposal, and over time the company becomes a model for corporate security in its industry.

Scenario 2: They love it. They agree to give you *carte blanche.* You implement every proposal, and over time the company begins to erode. Funding is gone, programs languish, the culture becomes hostile to security recommendations, and management turns to you and says, "Look at the damage you've caused!"

Scenario 3: They listen patiently, look you in the eye, and ask you to reconsider this plan, revise it, and bring them something they can accomplish. You leave the room knowing your credibility has taken a hit.

Which scenario you get might depend upon your company's degree of readiness.

Organizational readiness is an oft-overlooked but radically important element in strategic planning. Fortunately, it's a relatively simple concept.

In our movie analogy, the oppressed people who suffer an initial defeat generally lose because they are underprepared, they have fewer resources than the enemy, or they simply don't have the confidence to win. It can be the same with a company. If an organization is too financially strapped to invest in new programs, if its culture is anti-change or anti-security (e.g., if employees are used to a very open, permissive atmosphere), or if it has no experience with security programs the size and scale of what you're proposing, it may not be ready for your proposal.

This does not mean the company needs to change to fit your plans. You need to change to work with your company to provide the best programs you can under the circumstances, and hopefully your positive leadership will guide them into a position to implement stronger proposals down the road.

If your security strategic plans don't meet with the enthusiasm you expect, your organization may be telling you, "Look, we don't need another hero. We need a leader who will partner with this organization to set and accomplish realistic goals."

That doesn't mean you can't push the envelope; it doesn't mean you have to scrap the best security plan you can imagine. It just means you need to be aware of how ready your organization is for that grand plan, and you need to be ready to prioritize its elements, putting some portions on the back burner while you focus first on others.

CHAPTER 13

The New Security Assessment

By Robert D. Gates, security executive at a Fortune 100 company

What do security risk and threat assessments mean to you? Do you see them as your opportunity to justify the purchase of new technology? To present a list of existing solutions in place and their perceived effectiveness? To gain support for solutions that will help the business? Now, what do security risk and threat assessments mean to the executives and upper management to whom you present them? Are they opportunities for improvement, unwelcome requests for even more funding, or are they inconsequential?

How you view, conduct, and present security assessments determines how your upper management will perceive them and, often, whether they'll act upon your requests and recommendations.

Many of us have conducted security assessments by showing up with a clipboard that held a series of questions with Yes and No checkboxes next to them—Are our lights working? Are the locks operational? We filled it out and we handed it to our clients (the upper management or executives) as our final product. Those checklists deal with extremely important security issues like technology, regulations, crime, and liability. But are they the best vehicle to help us present security risks, threats, and solutions to our clients?

If your goal is to promote the security program by adding new technology or by getting management off your back, the checklist may be the best way to do it. It's also a good way to invite management to view security as a target for funding reductions and to view you as an inhibitor of the business instead of an enabler. This isn't because security isn't important to the business. It's because the checklist doesn't speak to your clients in their language. For example, if you walk up to the CEO of a bank, hand him or her the checklist and start talking CPTED (Crime Prevention Through Environmental Design), you're likely to get a polite smile or a blank stare, not because it's not a significant issue, but because it's not being presented in a way that enlightens the client or shows why it's important to the business.

On the other hand, if your goal is to promote the business, improve the business, and protect the revenue stream and the company's integrity, the checklist we've traditionally used is just your first step. It is a valuable tool for assessing the security of our businesses, but it should be just that—a personal data collection tool, not our final product. We still need to collect data on crime, incidents, and the reasonableness or effectiveness of our current solutions. But then we must take that information, consider the audience we need to reach, and develop an assessment that will speak to that audience, capturing the language they will understand and inspiring action. In order to get action from our audience, our assessment must:

Audit to expectations and standards
Adapt to business advantages
Achieve residual security benefits from ordinary business practices
Align with corporate goals
Articulate the business case

Here are a few tips on how to accomplish that.

- **Focus your assessment on business results.** Your final work product doesn't need to drill down to recommendations of specific technology items. Instead of presenting technology-oriented solutions, which are often viewed as unpleasantly high-cost recommendations, lay out the benefits and advantages your mitigation strategies will offer the business. For instance, can you present metrics that show how improved access controls or awareness programs would save labor or money? Can you achieve residual security benefits by hooking security's trailer to another ordinary business practice that already works for the company? Write and present your security assessment as a business case.
- **Think about your audience.** Determine who has the influence to execute the actions you're recommending. If you're the person who has that authority, then what you're proposing is really your personal objectives and initiatives for which you need your clients' buy-in or departmental funding. If your clients are the ones who must take the action, your assessment should be geared towards motivating them to act, explaining why they should, or focusing on

how to help them do their job better. Know your audience and take them into account early on so you know not only their objectives but how to craft and frame what you're going to say.

- **Watch your language.** While security professionals too often think in terms of cops and robbers, the business executives we're trying to influence think in terms of revenue and opportunities. The language we use in our assessments has to reflect that point of view if we're to get their attention. We need to highlight how the security strategy can lower costs or increase efficiencies, grow or protect revenue, and retain or attract customers.

    How we define certain familiar security terms is a prime example of this. For instance, the accepted definition of "crime prevention" from the National Crime Prevention Institute is "the anticipation, recognition, and appraisal of a crime risk and the initiation of some action to remove or reduce it." If you hand that definition to a business leader, it will not read in terms of how this concept affects business. But we can rephrase it to get their attention just by adding a couple of action items without changing the meaning: "the anticipation, recognition, and appraisal of a risk or opportunity and the initiation of some action to mitigate the risk or capitalize on the opportunity." Make sure to explain the opportunities and business objectives of every solution you propose.

- **Think strategically.** When assessing your efforts and results, ask yourself if what you are communicating represents a security tactic or a business strategy. Too often the security professional reaches for the comfort zone of tactics before considering the strategy. If we organize the security assessment to first sell a strategy, the tactical action will follow. When finishing the assessment, leave the check-lists behind. They only serve as your work papers, so presenting them as "the" assessment only serves to feed the security stereotype of a bureaucratic exercise.

The way we present security assessments, as well as the content they present, will help determine what our clients will be willing to do with them. It will also determine whether your upper management grabs their wallets when they see you coming or opens the door and offers you a seat at their table.

CHAPTER 14

Expect the Best: Evaluating Your Security Staff

With insight from Jim Hutton, director of Procter & Gamble's Global Security Division

A weak hiring process can cripple any business unit. If the chosen staff doesn't demonstrate the skills necessary to succeed in the function and in the business, then even a manager or executive with all the qualities of an effective leader will struggle to guide the department to excellence.

Numerous organizations, large and small, have recognized this fact and implemented processes to ensure that their business is built upon a solid foundation of skilled, qualified, and talented employees. Procter & Gamble (P&G), a global manufacturer of consumer goods, is among their number. With more than 138,000 employees in more than 80 countries, P&G recognizes the need to evaluate employees throughout the enterprise based on a common set of standards. The company has done extensive research to identify the "success drivers" or characteristics that typify high-performing employees, and from them has developed evaluation criteria for new and existing staff.

Jim Hutton, director of P&G's Global Security Division, explains that the Success Drivers concept "tips its cap to the internal equities we need to be mindful of when we recruit, train, promote and develop our people." Figure 14.1 shows the three general categories of criteria. The Power of Minds includes concepts like creativity, innovation, and decision making. The Power of Agility comprises flexibility and the ability to effectively meet change. And the Power of People incorporates ideas like leadership and collaboration skills. All managers are expected to use the Success Drivers process, which adds to the criteria a scoring system that helps them quantify how well each employee has incorporated the skills into their work.

According to Hutton, focusing on the behaviors that reside within the three categories increases the chance of success for both employees and managers within the company. "These things are important to the culture," says Hutton. "No matter what previous success someone has

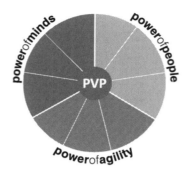

values
integrity . trust . ownership . leadership . passion for winning

Figure 14.1 The three categories of the Success Drivers concept.

enjoyed in a law enforcement or security career, if you don't do some of these things you're not going to make it internally."

When Hutton came to P&G through the company's acquisition of Gillette, he immediately recognized the value of P&G's approach to hiring, and decided to build upon it to enhance hiring decisions even further within the Global Security Division.

"I wanted best-in-class in terms of competencies to look for," says Hutton. As a member of the Security Executive Council, he became aware of a tool called the Next Generation Security Leader graphic (Figure 14.2). Figure 14.2 lays out six skill sets that are crucial elements of excellence in the security field: government elements, security organization elements, IT security elements, executive leadership skills, business elements, and emerging and horizon issue awareness.

Hutton approached his management about using these skill sets, in addition to the company-wide P&G criteria, as evaluation criteria for employees in his division. "When I shared the Next Generation Leader document with my management, including the chief human resources officer, they loved it. The HR leaders beyond headquarters use it to help me to evaluate the global security talent that serves their regions; they can really use this to do a 360-degree evaluation of the security staff."

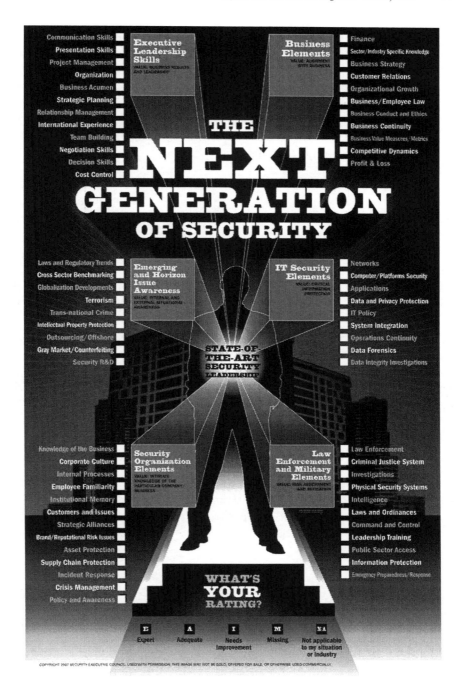

Figure 14.2 The six skill sets of the Next Generation Security Leader.

Hutton continues, "When we look for a new hire, we use the P&G process, and we layer that with the Next Generation Leadership competencies. When we have our quarterly performance reviews against agreed-upon objectives, we judge an employee's quarterly activities using those two same tools. Finally, when it comes time to promote someone, we again bring it back to these tools to make sure the competencies required by the new role are being developed by the successful candidate. It's an end-to-end utilization of the tools."

Using a system like this, in which expectations of all employees, and security employees in particular, are clearly laid out and communicated across the corporation, has a number of benefits. One is simply a stronger understanding, organization-wide, of what to expect of security roles, says Hutton. "I've shared [the Next Generation Leader criteria] with everyone in my organization, including the HR VPs in the regions, who were blown away by it. It helps them better understand what the security role is—what the competencies are from an external perspective—while building on the P&G Success Drivers. Some of them had never hired a security manager and didn't know what they were hiring, basically. This is a huge touchstone for them to be able to refer to."

This benefit applies to security employees as well. "People have become more thoughtful about what kind of roles they want to move into when they're offered a change of assignment, promotion, or the option to fill a vacancy, because they understand what the requirements are."

Transparency is another significant benefit. Says Hutton, "With mergers and people joining mid-career, there are always concerns about favoritism, or lack of opportunity. The Success Drivers and the Next Generation competencies are two things I can put in front of everybody and tell them where they net out against these two models. Not everybody likes it, but at least they all accept that it's transparent, objective, and applied consistently."

Take a look at your own organization's approach to hiring. Do you have a consistent and transparent method of ensuring you bring in only the best and brightest security employees available to you? Consider sitting down with your management to pinpoint the characteristics that are important to your corporate culture, and the characteristics you want to see in your security staff. It could help you build a stronger foundation for your function and your business.

CHAPTER 15

Business Evolution Requires Active Security Alignment

With insight from Dick Lefler, former VP and CSO of American Express and current chairman and dean of Emeritus Faculty for the Security Executive Council; and Greg Niehaus, professor of Finance and Insurance for the Moore School of Business, University of South Carolina

Business continues to change, and if the next generation of security leaders hopes to succeed, they must be prepared to change with it, says Dick Lefler, former VP and CSO of American Express and current chairman and dean of Emeritus Faculty for the Security Executive Council. This will require, among other things, a much more active pursuit of alignment with the organization's structure, goals, and strategies.

"What matters to the organization in terms of a risk management role is that you're identifying the risks that could either disrupt or enhance the organization's strategy," says Greg Niehaus, professor of Finance and Insurance for the Moore School of Business, University of South Carolina. "Alignment is important in that you want everyone in the organization to be thinking about and potentially identifying those risks." When the security leader is confronted with evolving business goals, evolving operational models, and evolving risks, such alignment can be more of a challenge than it has ever been.

"I think the next generation of security leaders is going to be faced with two significant risk issues to manage," says Lefler. "First, companies are doing business differently than they have in past generations. The next generation security director will have to demonstrate skills that not only are aligned to the business enterprise but that also reflect change in the way business is conducted."

The biggest change Lefler sees is an ongoing shift from a vertically integrated business model to a horizontally integrated one, meaning that fewer and fewer business functions are performed in-house. "From that point of view, a lot of your risk lies with somebody else's employees, goods, and services, and the ability to deliver those to you to further enhance or add value to the product and ultimately sell it. In today's competitive environment, you depend on others to provide raw resources, manufacture goods, and manage services like IT. The radical shift is that you're now managing risk relationships as opposed to managing the risks themselves," he says.

He offers the example of an electronics company that outsources its manufacturing. "If your manufacturer fails to provide you with adequate supplies based on your contract, you won't be able to sell as much product as you planned, and that will have a significant impact on your revenue and stock price," he says. "So part of that risk exposure may be the failure of your electronics manufacturer to adequately vet its employees or manage the risk in its own facilities." The security executive's responsibility in this case includes working with Legal to develop contracts that limit this risk exposure and to act as an agent of influence not only on his or her own senior management, but on the management of the contracted manufacturer. This expansion of responsibilities is just one of the elements of business alignment in an evolving risk atmosphere.

The second issue Lefler feels will most impact the next generation of security leaders is compliance. "Compliance in the global market-place is continuing to grow, and we're continuing to see sovereign nations work together to create increasing levels of compliance require-ments that carry with them penalties for failure to comply. The next generation of security leaders will have to be as sensitive to compliance as they are to the risk issues that can impact on the company. Failure to comply is a risk issue in and of itself."

Alignment in a changing risk and operational environment will require security leaders to actively engage management in an ongoing dialog, to ensure a shared understanding of business strategies and goals as well as identification of risks that are critical to the company and the board of directors.

CHAPTER 16

Emerging Issue Awareness

With insight from Dick Lefler, former VP and CSO of American Express and current chairman and dean of Emeritus Faculty for the Security Executive Council

Emerging issue awareness is perhaps the most difficult to define and the most difficult to obtain of all the knowledge areas the next generation security leader must master. It isn't taught at universities or learned by mentoring, it means something different in every company and industry, and upper management is looking for it now more than ever.

The term emerging issue awareness doesn't appear in lists of job qualifications or requirements, but it is often there, hidden in other language. Where a job calls for a "strategic thinker," someone "able to anticipate," who is adept at "planning for current and future needs" and "meeting the needs of a changing business environment"—there it calls for the elements of emerging issue awareness.

Being aware of emerging issues affecting the security of the company means making sure your senior management is never caught by surprise. It means keeping tabs on happenings and changes within the company; its industry; the security industry; business in general; technology; crime; local, national, and global politics and threats; and any other arena that could impact the organization.

This may sound like a lot to expect of the security executive, but to successfully provide security in today's business and economic environment, this skill set is a necessity. Threats can come at an organization from any angle or direction, and lack of preparation for them may cause extremely damaging financial, reputational, and safety issues.

Dick Lefler, former VP and CSO of American Express and current chairman and dean of Emeritus Faculty of the Security Executive Council, pinpoints several historical examples that illustrate the wide range of emerging threats the next-generation security leader must prepare for. On one hand, he points to the affects of 9/11 and Hurricane Katrina on companies that maintained current, tested business continuity and crisis response plans and those that did not. In this case, the CSO who kept up with the best practices of the security industry and the potential impacts of terrorism or natural disasters was able to provide his or her company a higher level of business protection and safety.

On the other hand, he highlights a single, seemingly minor technology evolution: the development and improvement of the color copier. When this device improved to the point that reproductions were indistinguishable from the originals at first glance, it changed counterfeiting from a sophisticated crime that could only be perpetrated with specialized equipment, to something that could be done by anyone with a quick trip to Kinkos. "In this case," says Lefler, "the CSO's familiarity with technology trends is what allows him or her to prepare countermeasures to meet an emerging threat."

The security leader's emerging issue awareness should encompass not only external concerns, but also changes within the corporation. If the business is getting ready to outsource, offshore, change packaging, or embark on joint ventures, mergers, or acquisitions, or even if there's a drop in sales, the security leader has to be aware of these potential changes. Then he or she must determine what those changes will mean to security and how best to respond.

16.1 CHALLENGES TO EMERGING ISSUE AWARENESS

Ten years ago, if we wanted information on the happenings in a certain area, company, or industry, we often had to scrounge to find it. Now we're buried in it. The Internet presents an overwhelming amount of information to the security leader searching for issues that may impact his or her company.

Maintaining constant watch over such a wide variety of potential risks and threats in a constant flood of data is a challenge that can be overcome through discipline and organization, as we'll discuss below. But recognizing within that sea of information which issues constitute emerging risks is a matter of experience combined with aptitude. Unlike some of the other knowledge areas we've discussed in this series, emerging issue awareness cannot be learned through academic programs, books, or other sources of training. It requires the security leader to train him- or herself over time to quickly identify significant issues as they develop.

16.2 TIPS FOR STAYING AWARE

There are myriad sources of information you can monitor to keep watch for issues that may impact your company. Industry associations, corporate public relations and investor relations departments, magazines, television stations and newspapers, government organizations, and research groups all offer services that help keep you up to date on the events that matter to them, in the form of e-newsletters, RSS feeds, news services, blogs, and websites.

The security leader's first challenge is to choose the right sources. Knowing your business and your security program, as well as your industry and the regions in which your company operates, will be crucial to choosing well. Sometimes this also requires creative thinking. Lefler explains that sometimes the best way to forecast and prepare for threat trends is to keep an eye on other industries that don't seem to have much to do with your own.

For instance, he says, if you're in pharmaceuticals and you anticipate problems with counterfeiting, you can learn something by watching how luxury goods manufacturers deal with their counterfeiting problems and then picking out the elements of their solutions that would be useful in your context. Similarly, if your company puts you in charge of protecting two million acres of timber and you find you have a timber theft problem, you can look to unmanned aircraft technology developed by the military for defense purposes to help you patrol the company's property. "Part of the CSO's job," says Lefler, "is to understand how to bring cost effective solutions to emerging threats by looking at what's going on in other sectors and converting that to your own thinking."

Once you've chosen relevant sources of information and subscribed to their services, the next challenge is sorting through all the e-mails, feeds, sites, and mailings to find the news that's meaningful for you and then to identify patterns and interpret the trends you see. It's important to remember that each source has a different slant on the news they provide.

If you want to avoid buckling under the weight of all this information, you must develop good habits and practice constant self-discipline. Here are some tips for handling the information overload.

- **Scan everything.** Learn to glance through magazine, e-news, and newspaper headlines and to get the gist of the story without stopping to read every word. Speed reading courses can bring real value.
- **Consolidate.** Avoid single-source documents or mailings; focus instead on news scanners, which pick out headlines based on criteria you set and only send you information that might be useful to you.
- **Organize.** Keep a separate e-mail folder for group mailings so that these items don't clog up your regular inbox. But set aside time every morning to scan through the folder and clear it out. Don't let it pile up.
- **Ask for help.** If you don't think you can do all this sorting and organizing by yourself, appoint a staff member to help you cull through the information. Another option is to partner with an analyst group that searches news based on your criteria and notifies you about items that are actionable or critical.
- **Network.** In your profession and across sectors, be prepared to be a fast follower on new ideas and solutions.

CHAPTER 17

Planning for Change

With insight from Mark Lex, former director of security for Abbott Labs and Security Executive Council faculty member; Bill Phillips, vice president and chief security and safety officer for CAN; Jeff Woodward, senior manager of global environmental health, safety and security for Panduit Corporation; and Bruce Meglino, professor of Organizational Behavior and Management at the Moore School of Business, University of South Carolina

"You have to create a strategic plan knowing that there's a high likelihood it will change. Does that mean you shouldn't plan? Absolutely not," says Mark Lex, former director of security for Abbott Labs and Security Executive Council faculty member. Over his career, Lex learned through hard-won experience that security strategic planning, done well, incorporates a balance of anticipation and response, detail, and flexibility.

In today's business landscape, that balance is extremely difficult to strike. Perhaps that's one reason so few security and risk leaders succeed at effective strategic planning, and so many don't plan at all. Here are some other possibilities.

1. **They don't understand it.** There are plenty of capable leaders out there who didn't go to business school and who have never been asked to create strategic plans for their security departments. They are intelligent and motivated, but learning about strategic planning is simply not a priority, so it goes undone until management requires it. Then, under the gun, they create plans that demonstrate their lack of knowledge. "A lot of people don't understand the basics of what strategy is," says Lex. "It gets confused with goals. The goal is what you're planning to accomplish. The strategy is the how-to—how you are going to accomplish it."

2. **They've mystified it.** Security strategic planning is no different from strategic planning in any other business function. Yet, because security leaders (and business leaders as well) have only

in recent years begun to look at security as a business function, common practices like strategic planning have retained an other-worldly aura. Security is viewed as special or different—meaning exempt—because the function regularly conducts risk analyses and attempts to predict risk outcomes, making the SWOT (strengths, weaknesses, opportunities, and threats) analysis included in strategic planning seem redundant. In short, strategic plans seem at best inaccessible, at worst irrelevant.

3. **They don't know where to learn it.** Security leaders with a business background are likely to be familiar with the basics of strategic planning. Bill Phillips, vice president and chief security and safety officer for CNA, learned by running his own consulting business. "If we didn't have strategies for our business plans we just wouldn't have been successful," he says. Those without such experience may not know where to turn.

    Libraries—particularly university libraries—generally have some good resources. A very few security seminars and leadership programs offer some strategic planning guidance. "I went to GSO 2010 several years ago," says Jeff Woodward, senior manager of global environmental health, safety, and security for Panduit Corporation. "That seminar really opened my eyes to strategic issues." James Connor, one of the organizers of GSO 2010, subsequently acted as consultant on a large project for Woodward, and he assisted in developing strategic plans to incorporate that project's results.

    And then, there's always trial and error. "I learned by getting shot down enough times and going back to the drawing board enough to begin to figure out what I was doing wrong," says Lex. "Then I studied up and called upon colleagues and peers, contrasting and comparing with what they had done and beginning to develop some of my own ideas."

4. **They don't take the time to do it.** "I'm a very technical person, so it was hard for me to push myself away from day-to-day operations and delegate more in order to have the time to create a strategy," says Woodward. This is a common challenge, particularly when so many security leaders are being asked to do more with less—money, staff, and time. However, having that well-developed strategic plan in place will pay dividends on the investment of hours and effort.

17.1 STRONGER INFLUENCE AND BETTER SECURITY

By all accounts, a good strategic plan will earn the security leader credibility in the eyes of senior management. They are more likely to trust someone who has been proven a strategic thinker, and they will be more apt to ask him or her for counsel. The career implications of this boost can't be overstated, and neither can its impact on organizational protection. A leader with the ear of management is in a better position to propose and win support for far-reaching, security-enhancing initiatives.

The benefits of strategic planning also extend to the rest of the security staff and the strength of the entire function. "[My strategic plan] brought unity to the group that I was leading," says Lex. "There was a common language, goal, purpose, and really a common how-to in our approach. It helped tremendously in the cohesiveness of the group."

"It helps to develop the people within the department at all levels," states Panduit's Woodward. A good strategic plan is communicated all the way through the ranks and (directly or indirectly) sets performance expectations for each role, says Woodward. "It improves individual employees' performance in their jobs and makes the entire department stronger." In the long run, this all means better security.

Other benefits might include improved continuity during leadership changes (the management-approved plan gives new security leadership a point of reference for program development and focus) and support for staffing decisions (employee X is promoted over employee Y for her consistent contribution to meeting the department's documented strategic goals).

These benefits, of course, are only attained when the strategic plan is well-crafted. Some security professionals who jump the first hurdle and endeavor to write strategic plans miss the mark on the quality of the plans they develop.

If a strategic plan is written in such a way that it cannot be approved, or that it cannot be followed, or if the writer doesn't actually intend to follow the plan but is only writing it to appease the boss, its utility will be limited, to put it lightly. In fact, it may do more harm than good. Focusing on two sometimes-neglected aspects of strategic planning might help avoid these pitfalls: alignment and flexibility.

17.2 ALIGN, ALIGN, ALIGN

A security strategic plan, like a strategic plan in any business function, must line up with the organization's strategic plan. The importance of this cannot be overstated. "Our goals have to be in line with the company's goals, because our main purpose is to support and enable the business," says CNA's Phillips. "So our strategies support and mirror the corporation's strategies. That's the first thing security folks need to get out front on." Because CNA's business, as the country's seventh-largest commercial insurance writer, is in risk and providing a marketplace for risk transfer, its security function draws goals and strategies around how to enable the business to be more effective and efficient in that mission. Phillips explains, "We examine operational risk, so our strategies are how we identify, examine and work with the risk the organization faces."

Alignment need not end with the organization-wide strategy, emphasizes Woodward. "The thing that's helped me the most is aligning to everything possible in the organization—core competencies, smart goals, service to employees, EHS programs, the lean program. We've aligned to our marketing strategy for our product, and that's helped a great deal in pushing our plans through and getting our capital approved."

Aligning means keeping connected to what the business is doing at all times. When the business changes or its plans change, an aligned function will ensure that its corresponding plans will change if necessary to remain aligned. This is where flexibility comes in.

17.3 SECURITY AS A NIMBLE FUNCTION

The U.S. and international recessions, multiple wars, terrorism, and political uncertainty have caused businesses worldwide to hunker down, says Bruce Meglino, professor of Organizational Behavior and Management at the Moore School of Business, University of South Carolina. "Generally as things become more uncertain, organizations take a shorter-term view because they're not sure what's going to happen. Organizations abhor uncertainty," he says.

Security strategic plans must be flexible. "We need more anticipation, we need more business knowledge, and we need more nimbleness," says Lex. "The business executives who are best at strategy tend to design their strategies with several options. They're not willing to ride one strategy into the ground and crash and burn because it isn't working anymore. If they see their strategy isn't working, they apply some nimbleness and shift the strategy.

"For instance, you can lay out your budgeting based on last year's budget, but you also plan for a 30% contingency and a 50% contingency. In other words, what are you going to be able to provide to the organization if your budget's cut in half or cut by a third?" asks Lex. This helps the security department shift gears quickly if the budget cuts come to pass, and in some instances it also helps the security leader defend against those cuts. If the executive staff asks the security leader whether they could expect the same level of service under such cuts, the security leader has an honest and documented answer prepared in his or her strategic plan.

Some security organizations have been successful by planning strategy at a less granular level in order to accommodate changes that impact the business direction or budget. This method must be used carefully, however, because if the strategy becomes too high level, it may become vague and lose its ability to provide practical guidance.

The good news is, flexibility is one area in which security functions should have an advantage in planning.

"For security to be effective, we have to be forecasting," says Phillips. Monitoring and analyzing intelligence can serve the dual functions of risk management and business alignment through strategic planning, he says. The security function that is already collecting and analyzing intelligence on risks that may impact the business is more equipped to predict (and prevent where possible) business-changing events. In addition, security more than other functions should recognize the value of backup plans and business continuity.

17.4 EFFICIENCY VS. FLEXIBILITY

Flexibility in strategic plans is valuable, but it must be paired with an ability to change quickly enough to follow revised plans or goals. Meglino remarks that there are steps organizations can take to increase their potential flexibility.

Before considering them, Meglino cautions, organizations must understand that increased flexibility inherently makes organizations less efficient. "The most efficient way to manufacture an automobile is on an assembly line," he explains. "Extremely efficient, but very difficult to change because they're specifically designed for that one purpose. There's a constant trade-off that organizations need to make between efficiency and flexibility."

The structural design of companies can make them more efficient or more flexible. "For example," says Meglino, "centralized decision making is usually thought of as having greater potential for efficiency, but it is very inflexible. Think about McDonald's compared to a local restaurant. McDonald's is very efficient but very inflexible. You can't walk in there and say, 'Let me have a hamburger with an egg on it.' They don't know how to react to that because it's not part of the protocol. A local restaurant, on the other hand, can be flexible enough to give you what you're asking for."

Hiring practices can also impact flexibility. "If you hire people with very specific talents targeted exactly to the job they're supposed to be doing, you're hiring for efficiency but not flexibility," Meglino continues. "If you set up cross training in an organization to allow employees to become broadly familiar with things beyond their job, that's an investment, as is hiring people with multiple skill sets. It's costly, but it increases the possibility that your organization is going to react to changes in its environment more successfully."

Security leaders who carefully craft aligned, flexible strategic plans will reap the benefits of increased influence, greater effectiveness, and stronger departmental unity. If you haven't yet been asked by management to present your security strategic plan, don't wait. Begin now and ask trusted peers within and outside the business to assist you.

CHAPTER 18

Reinventing Security

By Chris Berg, senior director of corporate security and safety for Symantec Corporation

Successful leadership of any business function relies upon an understanding of the organization, the function itself, the culture, and the team. After a few years at the organization, you're able to internalize that understanding, so when changes come along, you can easily draw upon it to aid in decision making. In some instances, however, you're not allowed that benefit of time and hard-won understanding to deal with sweeping changes, and this creates a unique challenge.

18.1 COMMON CIRCUMSTANCES OF REINVENTION

Over the past 20 years, I have helped to lead what I call "reinventions" of several security functions. Reinventing security entails quickly working through drastic organizational changes or functional flaws to create a new function that meets the needs of its business.

There are at least four common circumstances that call for reinvention of the function:

- **A shift of focus in an existing function.** This may happen when an organization decides to pursue the convergence of physical and logical security, or when legislation or standards require changes in the governance of the function, for example. A shift of focus is generally the least demanding circumstance for reinvention.
- **Merger or acquisition.** Of course, when one business merges with or acquires another, the resulting new business will have a new risk and security profile, and previously independent security functions can merge or remain to some degree autonomous. The complexity of this type of reinvention will depend upon many factors, such as the sizes of the organizations, locations, cultural differences, and accepted security postures of the companies involved.
- **New functions in maturing organizations.** As organizations grow and their needs and risks change, they may create new security functions

for responsibilities that were previously handled informally or by other business units.

- **Broken functions.** Occasionally senior leadership will recognize that an existing function is not effectively mitigating the risks that are important to the organization, and they'll bring another resource to the table that might help them fix it. I believe this is the most difficult type of reinvention, because not only are you dealing with reinventing the function, you are often dealing with the dysfunction and legacy issues that mark the existing function.

18.2 MILESTONES TO REACH

When you're asked to lead any one of these types of reinvention, you'll have to create a strategy that makes sense for the circumstances and organizations involved. However, I have learned that it's helpful to try to reach the following key milestones in most reinvention scenarios. These aren't necessarily in chronological order; many should be worked on in parallel with others.

- **Understand the problem statement.** This is not only important for the leader of the reinvention effort, but also for the senior management. In the cases of mergers and acquisitions (M&A) and new functions, the problem statement may be fairly clear to most. In the case of a broken function, it can be a significant challenge. Organizations often know they have a problem but have a difficult time pinpointing a range of issues or dynamics within the organization that keep it from prospering. You as the leader may have to quickly examine and assess the function and discern the cause or causes of the dysfunction. That's a big hurdle to clear.
- **Understand the culture, business overview, and executive priorities.** In some instances you may need to work hard just to get a seat at the table to truly understand what the C-suite priorities are for a new function, but getting that seat is critical.
- **Assess the risks.** In the very short term (30−90 days), assessing risks across the enterprise may be a daunting task, perhaps not even doable. If at all possible, you should aim for a reasonable assessment of the risks to the organization at the enterprise level. Initially you may only have time to interview key stakeholders and assess little more than anecdotal evidence. A more robust process will need to follow as you mature your organization.

- **Understand your inherited team, service delivery, core competencies, and where each succeeds and fails.** It's key to understand the gaps between service delivery and your developing goals.
- **Reestablish broken relationships and "disinvites."** In the case of a broken function, one of the biggest hurdles to reinvention is reestablishing broken relationships and what I call disinvites—when security has basically been shouldered out of cross-functional or interdepartmental discussions, decisions, and processes because of legacy problems. You have to reestablish security's role in those things through increased communications and reaching out, but you also have to reestablish credibility. You often have to get everything else working smoothly again and running well for some time before credibility is truly effectively reestablished.
- **Develop a game plan.** Once you've assessed the organization and the function and discerned the gaps and their causes, you will be able to lay out the roadmap for the new, reinvented function. Some tips on developing an effective plan:
    - Articulate the value proposition to the people who need to hear it.
    - Plan for short- and long-term wins.
    - Tie everything to your strategy; operational effectiveness alone is not enough.
    - Make sure that the proposed solutions "fit" the enterprise.
    - Consider scale and sustainability.
- **Develop appropriate new relationships; plant seeds to build/rebuild processes.** Once I have a game plan in mind, I plant conceptual seeds especially in the C-suite, so that I can go back to what feels like familiar ground on my next visit with the executive.
- **Gain sponsorship.** All of this effort is wasted unless senior management and other business leaders understand and support the vision of the reinvention. Make sure that you articulate the value proposition to C-suite and to your new alliances across the organization, as well as to new and legacy team members.
- **Understand and remove obstacles.**

18.3 HOW TO LEAD REINVENTION

All the above-mentioned milestones require the leader of a reinvention to call up a whole bevy of skills to be successful.

- **Conceptual skills.** You must be able to see the enterprise as a whole, recognizing interdependencies between functions as well as political and social nuances. In my experience, you don't generally have the luxury of unlimited time and resources to work these things out. Sometimes you have only 45 to 90 days to assess, put the plan in place, design the team, and start the process of inventing your new organization. You have to use your time wisely, use your investigative skills, ask the right questions of the right people, and listen carefully to the answers. Get in front of the current team and pay close attention to what's going on with them, how they're interacting with people, and what their relationships are like.
- **Communication skills.** You have to be able to successfully sell your value proposition. You must understand the various audiences whose support you'll need, and you have to be able to speak to each and to highlight the aspects of your plan that are the most important to them.
- **Ability to establish and drive a sense of urgency.** Encourage your team members and allies to recognize the importance of the task at hand. The market segment of the organization(s) may make this job easier or harder. Most of my corporate life I've been in the field of high tech, where time to market for new products might be a matter of months. In this market, a sense of urgency can become imbued in all aspects of the business. On the other hand, in the pharmaceutical industry, where I've also worked, time to market is significantly longer. It would not be uncommon to have 10-year business plans. This sense of "time" often colors the operations in the whole organization. In this type of environment, instilling a sense of urgency may be a bigger challenge.
- **Ability to accurately evaluate talent.** This skill is key to reestablishing relationships and credibility. The first step to regaining credibility is getting smart people to the table: either refocusing some existing talent or recharging the organization with new people. I like to "draft high," that is, to find the most talented people I can, people with strong decision making skills, experience, and expertise, without regard to how exactly they'll fit into the organizational chart. That part will work itself out over time. If you can build the right team with the right talents, you can then empower them to take charge of the situation and to stay true to the core ideology and vision that your plan has set forth. As they work competently through issues and problems, they will by default begin to rebuild these broken relationships.

- **Willingness to allow your team both to succeed and to fail.** The team you put in place must feel empowered to make the decisions necessary to move the function forward. If you've drafted the right team, the failures they experience are likely to be of the minor variety. It may feel like a risk to turn over the reins entirely to a new team, but the right people will generally make good judgment calls. They understand security and are on board with a mutual vision.
- **Comfort with ambiguity.** When you reinvent a function, particularly when you're dealing with a broken function, you have to be willing to play in the gray space. Things do not easily fall into categories of black and white. When I get comfortable, which doesn't happen often, I know something is wrong. If you're comfortable, you're not innovating.

PART *3*

Looking Forward

CHAPTER 19

Security's Role in Corporate Social Responsibility

With insight from Francis D'Addario, former vice president of Partner and Asset Protection for Starbucks Coffee and Emeritus Faculty member of the Security Executive Council

If your board of directors and chief executive officer have begun asking you about social responsibility, you're not alone. The Security Executive Council has noticed an uptick in the number of security executives being asked to run corporate social responsibility (CSR) programs for their organizations.

A CSR imposes on the company policies and practices that help create positive social and environmental impacts and that show a commitment to both stakeholders and the community. For those of you being called upon, as well as those who see this as an opportunity to grow or advance your career, keep in mind that CSR programs mean more than reputation management. They can improve business continuity and employee morale as well as expand markets and increase profits. Don't think of CSR programs as just charity events; they should be business-driven strategies that also support social benefits.

19.1 WHY SECURITY?

Francis D'Addario, former vice president of Partner and Asset Protection for Starbucks Coffee and Emeritus Faculty member of the Security Executive Council, says that companies have only recently realized that CSR makes good business sense. D'Addario is the author of *Influencing Enterprise Risk Mitigation* (Elsevier, 2013), which deals with issues of social responsibility.

"Now companies, organizations, NGOs and government agencies are realizing that their ability to transparently deal with others advances their mission, and security is a fast follower of executive management strategy. Recognizing risk [to people and communities] and letting people know you intend to do whatever is reasonable to mitigate it really buys you a lot of trust and confidence," says D'Addario. "It's becoming a fast if not well-known differentiator for best-of-class businesses."

Security acts as an enabler for CSR programs, D'Addario says. "The security of an organization really depends on how it is perceived. To be locally relevant, the company needs to assess local risk—anticipating the needs and dependencies and conditions relevant to the health and well-being of the organization being in that community. And you can do this in such a way that you're recognizing what opportunities are out there as you're recognizing the risks."

19.2 WHAT'S IN IT FOR YOU?

Of course, participating in a CSR program can bring the satisfaction that comes in doing good for your community and/or environment. However, running a CSR program is a great way to demonstrate your ability to add value to the organization. As stated in a 2009 *McKinsey Quarterly* article,[1] there are a number of ways that CSR programs can add real value to the organization, and accomplishing any number of these will reflect strongly on your skills as a business leader:

- Gaining access to new markets
- Identifying new products and innovations or increasing differentiation in order to meet social needs
- Improving reputation to increase brand loyalty or ability to implement premium pricing
- Cost savings through environmental operations and practices
- Improving employee morale, lowering costs related to turnover
- Lowering risk through regulatory compliance and NGO demands
- Improving long-term supply chain viability
- Reducing local resistance in markets by gaining public support and engaging local communities
- Avoiding negative publicity
- Leadership development through participation in CSR programs

[1]Sheila Bonini, Timothy M. Koller, and Philip H. Mirvis, "Valuing Social Responsibility Programs," *McKinsey Quarterly*, July 2009: https://www.mckinseyquarterly.com/Valuing_social_responsibility_programs_2393.

19.3 HOW TO GET A CSR PROGRAM STARTED

Use your existing knowledge of running new risk management programs to guide you. A good starting point is the common risk management program development cycle:

- **Perform Assessment.** Get to know the current situation and what can be improved.
- **Define Objectives.** Helping the world is great, but the only sustainable program is one that also provides value to the organization.
- **Develop Strategy.** When looking for value, give thought to four possible areas of focus for a CSR program: the workplace, the marketplace, the community, and the environment.
- **Implement and Measure Performance.** Don't forget to measure results!
- **Review and Communicate Results.**

CHAPTER 20

Advances and Stalemates in Security

By Bob Hayes, former CSO of Georgia-Pacific and managing director of the Security Executive Council; and Kathleen Kotwica, PhD, executive vice president and chief knowledge strategist of the Security Executive Council

At the start of each New Year, we always find ourselves reflecting on who we are as an industry, what we're doing, and where we hope to be. The Security Executive Council's ongoing research and trending of security-related issues has shed light on some remarkable changes in the security industry in the last seven to ten years, many of which are driven by technology advances and shifts in the business environment.

Let's focus specifically on management, strategy, and leadership issues. Based on our research and our collaborations with senior security executives in all types of organizations, here are our thoughts on how security leaders have advanced and where they seem to have hit a wall.

20.1 ADVANCES

- More security practitioners are coming to their roles from varied backgrounds—not just military or law enforcement—which is gaining influence with senior level hiring managers who are looking for a role more inclusive of business skills in addition to security skills.
- More practitioners are beginning to infuse business theory and processes into every facet of their function.
- There is more interest in the business community in educating executive business leadership about security risk.
- We are seeing more security titles at the executive level and a higher level of executive interaction in many organizations.
- Risk is becoming a more common focal point for senior management, and they are communicating with security more about that risk.

- More practitioners are connecting the dots between security and the risks to each function of the organization, seeing the bigger picture and where their function resides within it.
- Security leaders are giving more consideration to aligning their services with the board-level (10-K) risks[1] that are critical to the business.
- More leaders are recognizing the need to brand or rebrand their security department—to reposition how the organization and executive leadership views security, its capabilities, and its actions and how security responds in a business manner to those views.
- Operational excellence is increasingly a focus of future-oriented security leaders. While most of the work we've seen is preliminary, we have worked with and heard from a number of practitioners who are hoping to develop quality management programs for their functions. (For more information, visit https://www.securityexecutivecouncil.com/spotlight/?sid=27289.)
- Similarly, more security leaders are noting and moving forward on the need to build credible measures and metrics programs for security.

20.2 STALEMATES

- Security practitioners continue to offer on-demand, ad hoc services in reaction to events, but not enough strategic, long-term programs that are built upon a solid understanding of the business, its risks, and opportunities.
- Although senior business management is now savvier about security risk issues, there has been little forward progress in their understanding of the security function's role in the business.
- While more practitioners are beginning the process of aligning their services with business goals, few are using this exercise to its full potential. Recognizing a business goal to increase revenue, a security practitioner may simply make a strategic statement that security will work with the business to increase revenue. However, this statement has limited value unless it's backed up by specific, actionable plans for accomplishing it.

---

[1]"10-K risks" refers to Form 10-K, an annual report required by the United States Securities and Exchange Commission of all publicly traded companies and any privately traded companies with more than $10 million in assets and 500 shareholders.

- A surprising number of practitioners cannot articulate or do not know exactly what resources their function consumes or their capacity for delivering those services. They can't quantify how many full-time equivalents (FTE) are dedicated to a given project or service, they don't know whether the business units that benefit from their services actually value them, and in many cases they cannot sit down and list all the services security performs and for whom.
- In a similar vein, practitioners and corporations are generally unable to calculate the total cost of the security services being consumed by the organization.
- Security practitioners often view their department as something different from all the other business units and feel that exempts the function from behaving as the other units do—measuring performance, quantifying value, delivering on strategy initiatives, for example. Increasingly, executive management disagrees.
- Many security leaders have reported that they continue to have little control over budget allocations and discretionary spending. There are many potential reasons for this, but one significant factor is security leadership's inability to effectively influence executive management and to justify the spending they feel is necessary.
- Rarely are security services communicated in terms of what risk they mitigate, and this causes gaps in staff and leadership understanding and investment in those services.
- While metrics are an increasingly hot topic, many of the security practitioners continue to count things rather than to provide true, meaningful metrics. Metrics are intended to influence and to tell a story. It's good to know how many laptops have been lost, but that number isn't a useful metric. The metric provides context and points to solutions.
- As an industry, we still fail to have research-based documentation that provides baselines and templates for successful security.

In too many organizations, security remains an antagonist or an afterthought. This amounts to more than a public relations problem. True, in some businesses the biggest issue is that organizational leaders simply can't or won't see the value in robust risk management. However, our observations have shown us that often the problem is that the security leader doesn't see himself or herself as a leader, so he or she sees no need or desire to grow as a leader or to take the initiative to innovate the program or learn the business.

If you're reading this book, it's likely you do want to strengthen or maintain the quality of your program. Do you consider yourself a leader? How much do you know about the inner workings of your business? When was the last time you created or monitored relevant metrics about your program's operations and return on investment (ROI)? How often does your top management ask your opinion? Can you articulate your strategy? What do you need to do in the next year?

CHAPTER 21

Addressing the Knowledge Transfer Gap

By Bob Hayes, former CSO of Georgia-Pacific and managing director of the Security Executive Council; and Kathleen Kotwica, PhD, executive vice president and chief knowledge strategist of the Security Executive Council

Adding business value. Getting a seat at the table. Running security like a business. Aligning security with the organization. These are the contents of the Holy Grail of security leadership. Everybody talks about them. Everybody wants them. But most security leaders view them as the stuff of legend—great for motivation, but unattainable in reality.

The industry as a whole has a grasp on the issues and many organizations have worked in recent years to help security leaders develop individual skills that get them closer to these goals, step by step. There is an abundance of magazine articles, certifications, and seminars with that aim, and industry associations continue to partner with business schools to help security leaders better understand business. Still, few manage to capture the designations of "business enabler," "executive influencer," and "security aligner." What's missing?

Business schools and industry business programs are perhaps the most useful existing resources pointing security leaders in the direction of success, yet they leave out an important element. Taught by business professors, they focus on helping security leaders understand business practices and speak the business language. But these programs fail to continue to the next stage: How do they marry business processes with the job of risk mitigation? How does security become a business unit in its own right?

Knowing how to talk business doesn't equate to an automatic understanding of how security adds value. It doesn't give security professionals the practical programs to implement to support the business. Like any other business unit, security must follow a process to attain true management support and align with business. This process includes documenting work efforts to show what security is actually doing on a day-to-day basis. It includes the often arduous task of meeting with all key executives of the business units to find out their plans and to discover the role security can play in their goals. It also entails holding business unit leaders accountable for their decisions on what risks are important to mitigate and at what level. This is the type of knowledge that has allowed the few truly aligned security leaders to reach their level of influence and success. But where do you learn how to do this?

Research conducted by the Security Executive Council has identified seven personas that most security leaders generally fall into. One of the first steps to learning how to move up this continuum is finding out which category you're in.

1. Those new to security or new to their industry
2. Those interested in learning the other side (an IT leader learning corporate security or vice versa)
3. Program creators/validators, who are creating or recreating programs due to changes in corporate leadership or strategy
4. Program facilitators, who have established security programs at a maintenance level, generally with limited resources
5. Urgent innovators/expanders, who have established programs and are responding to significant situations, yet looking toward emerging issues
6. Program expanders, who are expanding on existing boundaries and roles of security, thus advancing internal business alignment
7. Next Generation Leaders, who are working at an industry or national level. These individuals are rare. They are future oriented and work across many domains. They are aligned and are influencers in their organizations.

Many of the elite individuals who have reached Next Generation status are Tier 1 Security Leaders™ in the Council, but they make up a very small segment of current security leaders. We've spoken with them about how they reached their level of success, and in most cases it comes from a combination of understanding the corporate culture, organizational readiness, personal ingenuity and motivation, mentorship, strategic thinking, and great timing. Yet one of the questions we frequently hear from even these top-tier individuals is, "How do I teach my people to be more strategic?" Reaching a state of influence and alignment doesn't in itself give a person the ability to show someone else how to do so, and often at this level there is little time to show others how to get there.

Thus, there is a wide gap in the transfer of valuable knowledge to security leaders, and this gap is dangerous. It means that the rare organization that now has a Next Generation Security Leader in place may have to begin nearly from scratch once that individual retires, because no successor has been able to grasp the secrets to his or her success. It means that when the industry loses one of these few, it has to start over every time and simply wait for the next visionary to show up. It means our industry will never move forward.

21.1 SEVEN CHARACTERISTICS OF A KNOWLEDGE-SHARING PROGRAM

So what is our industry to do? If we can't address this gap, the practice of security can never move forward. Without the right training in place, every time a visionary security leader retires, his or her replacement has to start anew instead of building from the level of his or her predecessor.

Successful security executives are not going to be able to individually mentor every security and risk practitioner who wants to learn their secrets. We need a new breed of training program that can pass this knowledge along. We believe there are seven criteria this new type of knowledge-sharing program must meet.

1. **It has to have the right teachers.** Business professionals do an expert job of teaching business theory and practice, but a course cannot adequately address how risk mitigation should work within the business unless it offers equal instruction from individuals with personal experience in the security and risk fields. Our industry needs a program that is taught by business *and* security professionals, not business *or* security professionals.
2. **It has to be developed with input from practitioners.** It's true that sometimes we don't know what we don't know. But many security practitioners are very clear on the type of knowledge they need and the type of training they're not finding. An effective program will solicit input from the people on the front lines to inform the curriculum.
3. **It has to cover the subjects Next Generation Leaders must master.** Next Generation Leaders are those rare individuals, working at an industry or national level, who are future oriented, who work across many domains, who are aligned with the business, and who are

influencers in their organizations. While input from practitioners is one important aspect of curriculum development, it's also crucial that this new breed of program offer a curriculum that is built from a distinct and intimate understanding of the skills, characteristics, and processes that help make our most successful colleagues so successful.

4. **It has to begin by assessing each participant's leadership development and needs.** A course can't teach you how to move forward if neither you nor the instructors know where you are now. An effective course curriculum will begin by asking participants to think about and try to understand where they are in their organization, in their career path, and in their leadership development so that they can better understand what they need to learn.

5. **It has to guarantee that it will provide actionable information.** It's great to know how to talk the business talk. Now what are you supposed to do with that? That's the problem many existing programs have. A program that truly and effectively teaches "the business of security" will be one that gives participants tangible takeaways they can immediately begin to use in their organizations.

6. **It has to allow participants to continue to connect after the coursework is over.** Schoolteachers joke (some more seriously than others) that their participants always come back from summer vacation having forgotten everything they learned the year before. Once a class is over, it can be easy to go back to the grind and forget what you've been taught. An effective program will offer ways for participants to stay connected to the coursework after it's over by continuing to communicate with instructors or fellow participants.

7. **It has to be affordable.** The tuition for business school offerings can run into the tens of thousands, and in this economy even profitable multinational companies are balking at those prices. If a new training program is going to change our industry, it has to reach a lot of people, and the only way to do that is to make the program extremely affordable.

At the Security Executive Council, we want to see our industry transformed. We want to see a program that offers everything we've described here, because we think this type of training could help to elevate security to an executive concern across the board.

CHAPTER 22

Eleven Ways to Encourage Strategic Thinking

By Bob Hayes, former CSO of Georgia-Pacific and managing director of the Security Executive Council; and Kathleen Kotwica, PhD, executive vice president and chief knowledge strategist of the Security Executive Council

In Chapter 21, we discussed the dangerous knowledge transfer gap between visionary security leaders and the next generation of leaders who will succeed them. We also laid out a roadmap for a new type of training that would help to close that gap. But what topics do up-and-coming leaders need to know more about?

For years the Security Executive Council has worked with top-tier security leaders to develop research, track industry trends, and solve problems. In the course of this work, these Tier 1 Security Leaders have shared with us their thoughts on the skills that are lacking in the deputies and other potential leaders they are grooming. Most often they are concerned with the lack of strategic thinking and planning skills in these individuals. This shouldn't be surprising; many deputies have to work 10 hours every day on critical operational issues and have little time to devote to strategy.

We've identified 11 key strategic areas that Tier 1 Security Leaders would like to see their direct reports take on.

1. **Aligning board-level risk and business unit mitigation strategy.** The next generation of leadership will need to know how to line up their programs with the risk categories most important to the board of directors.
2. **Communicating hazards and risks, mitigation, and performance metrics.** Management and board members make critical decisions based on a host of spreadsheets, graphs, and trend lines. Effective, actionable risk management requires disciplined analysis. Security leaders who want to show their business-based contribution to the organization must know how to a) understand the data they're collecting to identify risks, and b) use that data to tell a compelling story of performance and value to the organization.

3. **Influencing community preparedness and resilience for emerging global risks.** Catastrophic manmade and natural risks will continue to threaten organizations and communities, making crisis and continuity management ever important. Security leaders need to be versed on the latest global requirements for preparedness compliance, and they must take steps to create community alliances to help build resilience and protect brand.

4. **Managing information protection, breaches, and situational intelligence.** Brand stakeholders require confidence. Information ranging from intellectual property assets to personal identifiers must be protected from persistent physical and cyber threats. The next generation of security leaders needs to know how to roadmap protection architecture and how to manage information crises at the speed of the Internet.

5. **Adding business value with mission assurance and profit and loss performance.** The successful security leader of tomorrow must understand both how to add value and how to show it. Risk mitigation is no longer just consequence protection. Security leaders need to demonstrate security's revenue influence and cost avoidance in return-on-investment calculations and operating statement results.

6. **Researching next generation organizations, programs, and leadership style.** Security leaders who understand their organization, its employees, and their own leadership development are in a strong position to accurately benchmark and gauge program success. They must learn the steps to evaluate themselves and their organizations against industry research to inform their role and corporate readiness.

7. **Governing compliance and social responsibility for brand equity.** The connection between ethical performance—including compliance and community care—and market performance is increasingly relevant. Research by the Ethisphere Institute shows that the most ethical performers are rewarded in the marketplace. How can security leaders play a role in stronger ethical performance?

8. **Conducting assignment, contract, hire, incident, and transaction diligence.** With estimated global occupational fraud exceeding $3.5 trillion[1] in 2012 and identity theft at epidemic levels, organizations

---

[1] Association of Certified Fraud Examiners, "2012 Report to the Nations: Key Findings and Highlights," http://www.acfe.com/rttn-highlights.aspx.

need multi-factor authentication of persons, cargo, conveyances, and information. Errors, omissions, and fraud are increasingly discoverable with well-integrated and layered security solutions that will likely be required by evolving compliance.

9. **Transferring risk mitigation competence.** Risk mitigation has become increasingly cross-functional; it's important for security leaders to know how to identify, develop, and retain talent at all levels for sustainable results. Ongoing risk assessments must be included in project and program management along with continuous education and training.

10. **Building strategic brand alliances and community.** Public and private community partnerships with clients, governmental agencies, peer organizations, and trade associations can augment the in-house resources. Security leaders need to know how to build these partnerships and to sustain them for the greatest benefit to all.

11. **Applying proven practices and solution innovations.** Innovative solutions can lend confidence to common risk situation management. Solution evaluation should include pilots that allow for the measurement of cost savings, loss avoidance, and opportunity improvements. Proven solutions should optimize core organizational processes and outcomes.

CHAPTER 23

Risk at High Velocity

With insight from Francis D'Addario, former vice president of Partner and Asset Protection for Starbucks Coffee and Emeritus Faculty member of the Security Executive Council

The next generation of security leaders will be challenged more than their predecessors to run the security function as a business; they will be expected to align with the organization and build value through security. As they work toward these goals, they will also be faced with new risks, some of which have the potential to escalate at a stunning pace.

For example, communication on the Internet has been a boon to business, but it has created an online environment that can be dangerous to corporate reputations. Consumers, employees, and often partners habitually share opinions and information through social media and viral posts to popular sites, which can turn a single person's comment one day into a media firestorm the next.

Some of you may remember when Alec Baldwin was kicked off an American Airlines (AA) flight in 2011 for reportedly verbally abusing the flight crew after refusing to turn off his phone when asked. It's interesting to note that within 30 minutes of Baldwin's first notorious tweet about the incident, AA had tweeted a response stating they were looking into the incident, and within 24 hours their Facebook page had been updated with a refutation of Baldwin's version of the events and a defense of AA's actions. The book is still open on the incident, but at the moment it looks like Baldwin may have come out the worse in this fight. Not all companies are able to deflect socially driven bad press in the same way. The damage that harmful YouTube videos, tweets, or Facebook comments can do to an organization's stock price can add up to millions of dollars in brand equity, and how these incidents are handled can either minimize or maximize that damage.

Of course, it will not do to focus on newer threats like online security while neglecting the basics. Burgeoning security leaders must remember that physical security remains critical in managing risk, and the increased value of information actually makes physical protection even more important than before in many cases. Information—intellectual property as well as private employee and customer data—is a high-dollar asset in itself. When the assets on which information resides are compromised, the damage is therefore compounded.

The healthcare industry may serve as a telling example. Privacy Rights Clearinghouse data recently showed that more publicly disclosed data breaches occur in the medical industry than in any other, and most of those are due not to hacking, but to loss or theft of portable data devices. The next generation security leader must be prepared to protect information and brand from cyber threats and physical threats to information assets.

Protecting not only information but the enterprise at large will also require a solid strategy for preparedness and resilience. "Brand confidence and loyalty are intrinsically tied to responsibility before a crisis," says Francis D'Addario, former vice president of Partner and Asset Protection for Starbucks Coffee and Emeritus Faculty member of the Security Executive Council. D'Addario evangelizes for security leaders to build preparedness and crisis management capabilities by, among other things, enhancing the social responsibility initiatives of the organization. A company's investment in social responsibility in the good times, enabled by strong security and risk management, allows the CEO to stand in front of the media and the community after a disaster and say with sincerity that the company cares about the community and is truly doing all it can to help. There is significant intangible value to that kind of sincerity, according to D'Addario.

Building local alliances and attending to global preparedness guidelines and regulations is also critical. Numerous partnerships and partnership organizations have arisen to assist individual communities in developing preparedness and response plans that leverage the resources and knowledge base of both the public and private sectors to better protect communities and the businesses that reside in them.

Threats and risks will continue to pick up speed, and the next generation of security leaders will need to be quick enough to build security functions that can match them—functions that rely on solid protection strategy as a foundation for nimble, resourceful, and creative response.

CHAPTER 24

What Will Security Look Like in 2020?

By Francis D'Addario, former vice president of Partner and Asset Protection for Starbucks Coffee and Emeritus Faculty member of the Security Executive Council; Bob Hayes, former CSO of Georgia-Pacific and managing director of the Security Executive Council; and Kathleen Kotwica, PhD, executive vice president and chief knowledge strategist of the Security Executive Council

Organizations are now more complex than ever before, and there's no evidence that the coming years will reverse this trend. Companies have adapted to succeed in a global and decentralized market economy, increasing reliance on vendors, suppliers, and contract staff for what were previously in-house operations. They have changed their internal structure to better compete in changing markets and a down economy, and they have learned to leverage new technologies to increase the speed of both communication and business.

This complexity has brought new risks that pose an ongoing security challenge, at a time when security is already arguably at a disadvantage. Many institutions still have not regained confidence following the decade of security shortfalls that began in 2001. Global markets and governments face continued uncertainty, leading many businesses to stop investing in new infrastructure and programs and to instead cut costs and staff in an effort to weather a storm that may or may not be coming. Yet if organizations do not develop or maintain a robust risk strategy, they could suffer stunted growth and loss of revenue.

24.1 HOW SHOULD SECURITY EVOLVE TO EXCEL IN THIS ENVIRONMENT?

Some organizations have accepted the challenge to push security toward value enhancement and stronger, more consistent protection through the rest of this decade. They're already giving the industry a glimpse of what security could—and, perhaps, should—look like in the next decade.

24.2 WHAT SECURITY 2020 COULD BE: A CASE STUDY

The CSO begins the day briefing the rest of the C-suite on mitigation opportunities that the company's unified risk oversight team is tracking. He helped provide the momentum to convene the first risk council that over the years has morphed into a diverse, cross-functional collaboration, gathering crucial and timely insights from across the company to both identify and address hazards earlier and better than previous siloed efforts.

The CSO is a business partner who is actively engaged in responding to key operational needs. His team proactively seeks alignment with the business' goals through regularly scheduled meetings with business unit leaders.

Once relied upon for heroic efforts to protect personnel and assets, the security function's strategies have evolved to incorporate relevant performance metrics, including compliance certainty and contribution to plan. Security owns or plays a pivotal role in a wide range of organizational priorities, such as sales and supply chain exception reporting. Conventional fraud detection and response are augmented with cost avoidance planning, brand reputation protection, and corporate social responsibility, including community disaster preparedness. Security consistently applies its unique perspective to help build process and value improvements into these other functions.

The function is also advancing integration capabilities for the entire organization and the industry by participating in technology test beds. Partnering with solution providers, selected locations model, test, and prove the effectiveness of integrated security technology elements. Data is shared with operators and vendor and integrator partners to influence product and process improvement. In some cases, security is using technology manufactured by its own company to influence both risk mitigation and revenue.

Collaboration is a hallmark of the unified risk mitigation security strategy. Security maintains multiple internal and external information-sharing partnerships with public and private organizations, and it also works to forge a strong link with the community through social responsibility and philanthropic efforts.

The CSO's voice is requested and heard by other senior leaders and the board because of his experience and focus on business integrity and value; but his function does not falter in his absence. Superior performance, excellent insight into risks on the horizon, and refusal to exploit fear, uncertainty, and doubt have restored the confidence of management and other stakeholders. Security focuses on mentorship of inter-generational talent and leadership development to ensure that the function's opportunity to influence is not lost when the CSO cannot make the call.

Determined leadership and the evolution of the security function have resulted in contributions to the bottom line, a strong organizational emphasis on the value of security, higher stakeholder engagement, and measurable improvements in negative security events and business resilience.

*****

While the example of the CSO in this case study is not company-specific, it is not hypothetical. Each of the elements that contribute to success in our illustration is in place today at one of several organizations with which we have worked.

24.3 ELEMENTS OF 2020 SECURITY

There are five important elements a security leader should aim to incorporate into his or her program if it is to approach the level of effectiveness and efficiency of the case study in the previous section.

1. **A focus on board-level risk**

   We've identified nine categories of risk that are commonly of interest to boards: financial, business continuity and resiliency, reputation and ethics, human capital, information, legal, regulation/compliance and liability, new and emerging markets for business, and physical/premises and product. Your board's concerns may differ from these, but this is a good place to start.

   Get to know and understand what risks your board is most concerned about to determine which ones have security components. Determine whether you can line up your existing security programs with one or more of those concerns. Once you've categorized your existing programs, look at the categories in which security has little or no impact and think about what you can do to provide value in those areas. Update your strategy to focus on programs that deal

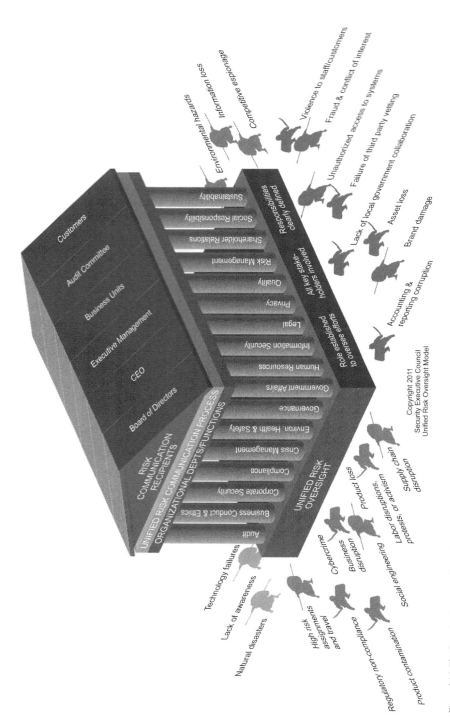

Figure 24.1 The Security Executive Council's Unified Risk Oversight™ chart.

with these risks, and then communicate your work clearly to senior management.

2. **Unified Risk Oversight™**

   Security does not "own" unwanted risks. Resilient organizations understand this and set up cross-functional groups to share information and oversight on risk issues. There should be many groups involved in risk oversight, including business conduct and ethics, compliance, legal, privacy, audit, and security (see Figure 24.1). Each of them owns or monitors some function that can provide detection or prevention of risk.

3. **All-hazards risk mitigation**

   Recognize that risk to the organization comes in myriad forms, many of which are not traditionally owned by corporate security functions. Risk mitigation need not confine itself to traditional corporate security risks; in fact, in many organizations, "risk" has been removed from corporate security's purview because of their traditionally narrow view. Risk must be viewed at an organizational level—high ground from which one can see and anticipate hazards of all types.

4. **Innovative integration**

   Programs exist that connect integrators, technology/service providers, and security practitioners for the purpose of testing and proving cutting-edge integrated solutions to provide a total security format with proven return on investment. This requires providers to focus on the needs of the 2020 organization rather than on product sales; organizations to open up the kimono and share metrics of product success; and integrators to step out of the comfort zone of a single product line and begin to think more creatively about integration options that could add value for their customers. If these three stakeholder groups in our industry collaborate in testing for improved interoperability, all will benefit.

5. **Inter-generational training**

   Our research shows there is a wide gap in the transfer of valuable knowledge to new and advancing security leaders. This means the next generation of security leaders is finding that in many respects they must begin anew when their predecessors retire or leave the organization, rather than building upon what their predecessors accomplished. Without training and mentoring in place, the security program will eventually take two steps back for every two steps forward.

About the Editor, Authors, and Frequent Insight Contributors

The following individuals contributed to the articles in this collection.

Dave Komendat is vice president and CSO at a Fortune 50 company. He has responsibility for the security needs of the commercial and defense sides of the business, in over 70 countries. Komendat's team is responsible for protecting people, property, and information, as well as for making the business resilient. His 2,000+ person team works to embed security and safety expertise within the business units, projects, and sales teams of one of the largest companies in the world. He is recognized as a strong industry and organizational leader and is involved in numerous professional organizations. He has received numerous industry awards. He is involved in the University of South Carolina's Darla Moore School of Business and its Risk and Uncertainty Management initiative, where he serves on the Board of Advisors.

Chris Berg is senior director, corporate security and safety for Symantec Corporation. Over the past 20 years, Berg has held numerous leadership positions in the high tech and biopharmaceutical industries. He joined Symantec in 2007. Prior to his corporate career, Berg served in the public sector as a supervising police detective in the San Francisco Bay Area and as a representative to California Department of Justice task forces. He has participated in the National Drug Control Policy Forum for the Executive Office of the President; the Transnational Threats Audit at the Center for Strategic and International Studies; and the Senior Executive Leadership Programs at Kellogg School of Management, Northwestern University, and Georgetown University. Berg has authored numerous articles on leadership and has been published in *Security Technology Executive* magazine, *Access Control & Security Systems* magazine, and *Security* magazine.

Marleah Blades has 15 years of experience as a professional writer and editor, including five as senior editor and manager of external relations for the Security Executive Council, where she was responsible for writing and coordinating feature articles and columns that share Council research and the insights of members, staff, and faculty for the betterment of the security industry as a whole. She also developed press releases and media announcements of news, products, and new research. She spent six years as managing editor of *Security Technology & Design* magazine, where she won awards for her coverage of trends and technology in the security industry. Blades holds a bachelor of arts in English from Pennsylvania State University.

Brad Brekke has held the title of vice president of Assets Protection for Target Corporation since 2001. Brekke leads a diverse team of executives with backgrounds in the public and private sectors in a comprehensive effort to mitigate risk, minimize loss and business disruption, and provide a safe and secure environment for Target and the communities it serves. He directs the Assets Protection division of Target, a Fortune 50, $62 billion corporation with over 300,000 team members, 1,700 stores nationwide, 30 distribution centers, 23 corporate facilities, and multiple overseas offices. Under Brekke's leadership, Target Assets Protection has developed strategic partnerships with law enforcement, emergency management, and public health organizations to continue to enhance Target's strong commitment to public safety and preparedness. A licensed attorney, Brekke formerly practiced in a Minneapolis law firm. Prior to that, he served as a special agent with the FBI, investigating complex cases involving financial fraud and public corruption.

George Campbell served until 2002 as the CSO at Fidelity Investments, the largest mutual fund company in the United States, with more than $2 trillion in customer assets and 32,500 employees. Under Campbell's leadership, the global corporate security organization delivered a wide range of proprietary services including information security, disaster recovery planning and crisis management, criminal investigations, fraud prevention, and more. Since leaving Fidelity, Campbell has served as a content expert for the Security Executive Council, of which he is a founding Emeritus Faculty member. Prior to working at Fidelity, Campbell owned a security and consulting firm, which specialized in risk assessment and security program management. He has also been group vice president at a system engineering firm that supported government security programs at high-threat sites around the world. Early on in his career, Campbell worked in the criminal justice system, and served in various line and senior management positions within federal, state, and local government agencies. Campbell received his bachelor's in Police Administration from American University in Washington, D. C. He served on the board of directors of the International Security Management Association (ISMA), and as ISMA's president in 2003. He is the author of *Measures and Metrics in Corporate Security* and contributing editor of *The Manager's Handbook for Business Security*.

Francis D'Addario has led cross-functional teams at Starbucks Coffee, Hardees Food Systems, Jerrico Inc., The Southland Corporation (DBA 7-Eleven), and Crime Prevention Associates. He is a co-developer of RED, an enterprise risk event reporting and analytics tool. D'Addario is an accomplished all-hazards risk mitigation practitioner and strategy leader. His influence and vision are credited with measured results for anomaly detection, asset recovery, business continuity, compliance, cost avoidance, crime prevention, information protection, investigations, operational auditing, policy governance, profit contribution, supply chain quality assurance, and team engagement. His executive committee experience includes audit, compliance, governance, and information security. His cross-functional protection and profit improvement methodologies have been featured by *America's Most Wanted*, *Christian Science Monitor*, CNN, *CSO*, *ISO Focus*, the *New York Times*, *Security Management*, and the *Wall Street Journal*. D'Addario has an Editorial Board appointment to *LP* magazine and has also served in volunteer leadership positions with ASIS, McGruff House, and The West Seattle Food Bank throughout his career. Professional recognitions include *Security*'s "Most Influential," *CSO*'s "Compass," The National Food Service Security Council's "Lifetime Achievement" award, and Jerrico Inc.'s "Manager of the Year." D'Addario publications include *Influencing Enterprise Risk Mitigation* (formerly titled *Not a Moment to Lose*).

Robert D. Gates was previously executive director, asset protection and corporate security, at AT&T. While in this role he was responsible for the delivery and execution of enterprise corporate security objectives and results to the AT&T family of companies. Since he first joined AT&T in 1984 (when it was known as Ameritech), he has advanced through a number of security roles, which included a wide variety of diverse roles and growing responsibilities. He has an undergraduate degree from Western Illinois University and a master's degree from Roosevelt University, and has instructed significant training and educational opportunities. He was a course developer and instructor for the telecommunications industry's basic investigation school for new investigators at AT&T and other national telecoms, and has experience as an adjunct instructor at his local junior college. He has published a number of security industry articles.

Bob Hayes is managing director for the Security Executive Council, a problem-solving research and services organization that involves a wide range of risk management decision makers. Its community includes forward-thinking practitioners, agencies, universities, NGOs, innovative solution providers, media companies, and industry groups. Backed by a faculty of more than 100 successful current and former security executives, the Council creates groundbreaking Collective Knowledge™ research, which is used as an essential foundation for its deliverables. The Council is the eminent voice on organizational risk mitigation leadership. Hayes has more than 25 years of experience developing security programs and providing security services, including eight years as the CSO at Georgia Pacific and nine years as security operations manager at 3M. His security experience spans the manufacturing, distribution, research and development, and consumer products industries as well as national critical infrastructure organizations. Additionally, he has more than 10 years of successful law enforcement and training experience in Florida and Michigan.

Jim Hutton, CPP, is the CSO and director of global security for the Procter & Gamble Company (P&G). He is the company's senior security executive responsible for worldwide security direction and consultation for all business units of this multi-billion-dollar enterprise that includes several iconic brands. His portfolio as P&G's leader of the People and Asset Protection Practice includes Global Security, Global Flight Operations, and Executive Meetings. Prior to joining P&G in 2005, Hutton worked as vice president and CSO for The Gillette Company of Boston, Massachusetts. He joined the company in 1993, and served in a variety of increasingly responsible security positions in the finance and administration areas. Prior to joining Gillette, Hutton was employed by the U.S. Department of State's Bureau of Diplomatic

Security for 10 years. Hutton was named the recipient of the Compass Leadership Award from the Chief Security Officer Organization in March 2008.

Rad Jones is an instructor in the School of Criminal Justice at Michigan State University, where he teaches a master's level course in Public-Private Partnerships in Homeland Security and Emergency Preparedness. Jones is part of the leadership team for the newly formed Business Continuity Alliance formed by MSU and the Security Executive Council. In 2000, under an Office of Justice Programs grant he published the Critical Incident Protocol—A Public and Private Partnership. Jones retired as the manager of security and fire protection at Ford Motor Company, where he was responsible for global activities in investigations, executive security, security guard administration, and fire/security alarm technology. He was instrumental in the development of a global risk assessment process, creation of crisis management teams, emergency response and disaster recovery programs, and a global security/fire central communication center. He retired from the U.S. Secret Service in 1983 as the special agent in charge of the Michigan division. He was recognized by *Security* magazine as one of the 25 most influential persons in security.

Mike Kalac is vice president and chief information security officer (CISO) of Western Union, responsible for all aspects of Western Union's global security strategy and information risk management program. Kalac is responsible for the development and execution of the enterprise-wide information security strategy and driving implementation of security-related programs within the business. He is also responsible for development and implementation of corporate security control policies and standards, as well as ensuring the appropriate tools and metrics are in place to allow for effective monitoring, measurement, and control of risk as it relates to information security and PCI compliance. Prior to becoming the CISO for Western Union in 2006, Kalac served for 11 years as the vice president of network engineering for First Data Corporation, Western Union's prior parent company. Additionally, Kalac held senior positions with such companies as McCaw Cellular One, Octel Communications, and Hewlett Packard Corporation. Kalac received his Master's of Business Administration from the University of Denver's Daniels School of Business and his Bachelor's degree in Electrical Engineering Technology from Texas A&M University.

Greg Kane is director of IT and product technology for the Security Executive Council. Kane is responsible for maintaining and enhancing the Council's software applications and technical infrastructure, and analyzing and mitigating risk as it applies to the Council's IT systems and the intellectual property assets contained within. Kane also serves as the chief technical design architect for the Council's IT systems as well as for the technical solutions provided to the Council community. Kane applies his 25+ years of experience in computer science, project management, and business consulting to ensure that technical solutions not only present an optimal application of relevant technology but that they meet real business needs in a cost-effective, timely, and practical manner. He has held lead roles in designing, implementing, and maintaining large complex applications for various businesses. His management experience includes leading multinational teams made up of employees, contractors, and third-party vendors in local and remote locations. Kane's educational background includes an MS in Computer Science and an MBA.

Lorna Koppel has been the VP, chief information security officer (CISO), for Iron Mountain since January 2013. Her role is designed to bring focus to growing information security needs and to deliver an effective global program to protect Iron Mountain's proprietary and confidential information, customer information, and technology infrastructure. Koppel has an extensive background in information security with over 20 years' experience in security and systems administration, risk analysis, and the implementation of high-profile global strategic initiatives. Throughout her career, she has worked closely with senior leaders and cross-functional teams to develop and execute strategic and tactical security programs, as well as develop strategies to address regulatory compliance mandates and other security-related requirements. Prior to joining Iron Mountain, Koppel was the CISO for global consumer goods manufacturer Kohler and director of global security at network service provider BT/Infonet Services Corp. She holds degrees from Bowling Green State University, Pennsylvania State University, and the State University of New York at Albany. In November 2010 Koppel was recognized as one of the industry's "Most Influential People in Security in the area of Information Technology/ Cyber Security Practitioners" by *Security* magazine.

Kathleen Kotwica, PhD, is EVP and chief knowledge strategist for the Security Executive Council, a business risk problem-solving research and services organization. Kotwica's responsibilities include establishing short- and long-term knowledge management strategies to maximize the Council's innovative output and uphold its mission to the Council community. She leads the development and production of Council tools, solutions, and publications. She also oversees online initiatives and marketing communications. In her role, Kotwica maintains the strategic goals and direction of the Council. She additionally conducts industry research and analysis to further security and risk management practices. Kotwica has a PhD in Experimental Psychology from DePaul University in Chicago. She has co-authored scientific peer-reviewed journal articles and has authored or edited many security industry trade and business magazine articles. She has spoken at several security-related conferences including CSO Perspectives, SecureWorld Expo, ASIS, and CSCMP.

Dick Lefler retired as the vice president for worldwide security of American Express in 2001. In addition to his security duties, Lefler managed the Corporate Aviation Unit. His responsibilities included program development and management of the security of employees, facility protection, investigation of attacks on financial products, and coordination with federal, state, and international law enforcement agencies regarding security concerns. Prior to joining American Express, Lefler was deputy special agent in charge of the U.S. Secret Service's New York office. His 20-year career at the Service included assignments as special agent in charge of protective operations, special agent in charge of the Honolulu office (Far East), and investigative and protective assignments in Los Angeles and Washington, D.C. In the nation's capital, Lefler's protective assignments included the Presidential Protective Division and the Vice Presidential Protective Division. He retired from the Secret Service in 1985 as a member of the senior executive service. Lefler received his undergraduate degree from the California State University, Los Angeles, in June 1964. He attended the Federal Executive Institute (Charlottesville, Va.), for Executive Education Program in 1981, and the John F. Kennedy School of Government's Program for Senior Managers in Government at Harvard University in 1982.

Mark Lex specializes in business programs and strategy development; strategic partnerships and alliances; and performing risk mitigation services for a wide range of large-, mid-, and small-size companies. Lex has worked as a business developer and consultant and continues to maintain Emeritus Faculty status with the Security Executive Council. Specifically, Lex develops operational risk strategies and programs, authors articles for members and the security profession, and coaches chief security officers. Lex spent 15 years as the top security executive for several Fortune 500 organizations. Lex was the director of global security for Abbott Labs, the director of safety and security for W.W. Grainger Inc., and the director of corporate security for Kraft Foods North America. Before joining the corporate ranks, Lex owned and operated several different investigative agencies and security officer companies in suburban Chicago. Lex is a former investigator with the Du Page County State's Attorney in the Chicago area, where he was assigned to the Special Prosecutions Unit. Lex holds a bachelor's degree from Western Illinois University in Law Enforcement Administration and Political Science and received his Master's in Security Management from Webster University, where he was named as a distinguished graduate.

John McClurg serves as vice president and chief security officer of Dell's Global Security Organization. McClurg's responsibilities include the strategic focus and tactical operations of Dell's internal global security services, both physical and cyber. He is also charged with the advocacy of business resilience and security prowess generally, the seamless integration of Dell's various security offerings, and with improving the effectiveness and efficiency of security initiatives. Before joining Dell, McClurg served as the vice president of global security at Honeywell International; Lucent Technologies/Bell Laboratories; and in the U.S. Intelligence Community, as a twice-decorated member of the Federal Bureau of Investigation (FBI), where he held an assignment with the U.S. Department of Energy (DOE) as a branch chief charged with establishing a cyber-counterintelligence program within the DOE's newly created Office of Counterintelligence. Prior to that, McClurg served as a supervisory special agent within the FBI, assisting in the establishment of the FBI's new Computer Investigations and Infrastructure Threat Assessment Center or what is today known as the National Infrastructure Protection Center within the Department of Homeland Security. McClurg also served, for a time, on assignment as a deputy branch chief with the Central Intelligence Agency, helping to establish the new Counterespionage Group, and was responsible for the management of complex counterespionage investigations. He also served as a special agent for the FBI in the Los Angeles Field Office, where he implemented plans to protect critical U.S. technologies targeted for unlawful acquisition by foreign powers and served on one of the nation's first Joint Terrorism Task Forces.

McClurg was recently voted one of America's 25 most influential security professionals, was a 2008 CSO Compass Award recipient, holds a J.D. from Brigham Young University, is a member of the Utah Bar Association, co-chairs the Overseas Security Advisory Council (OSAC) of the U.S. Department of State, and sits on the FBI's Domestic Security Alliance Council (DSAC). He also holds an MA in Organizational Behavior, and BS and BA degrees in University Studies and Philosophy from Brigham Young, and advanced doctoral studies in Philosophical Hermeneutics at UNC-Chapel Hill and UCLA.

Joe Nelson is AVP strategy specialist at State Street. He has over 20 years of organizational security and risk management experience within global companies. Nelson began his career over 30 years ago at Digital Equipment Corporation and has held a variety of executive level security and risk management positions with companies including IBM, Teradyne, CMGI, and Lotus Development Corporation. Nelson's specialties include design and development of security programs, design and development of contingency programs, security function performance (dashboard and metrics), conducting risk assessments, crisis and incident management, investigations, executive protection, physical security, strategic business planning, and technical programs. Nelson is a board Certified Protection Professional (CPP) and a contributing author to the *Handbook of Loss Prevention and Crime Prevention*, fifth edition, and was voted one of the top 350 leaders in the 2007 *Security* magazine Global Security Survey.

Greg Niehaus is professor of Finance and Insurance at the University of South Carolina's Darla Moore School of Business. He received his PhD from Washington University in 1985, and held faculty appointments at the University of Michigan and Michigan State University. He has served four years as senior associate dean for research and academics and four years as Finance Department chair at the Moore School of Business. His research has been published in *Journal of Financial Economics, Journal of Finance, Journal of Business, Journal of Financial Intermediation, Journal of Banking and Finance, The Accounting Review, Financial Management, Journal of Financial Services Research, Journal of Risk and Insurance,* and *Financial Analysts Journal.* His current research interests include corporate finance, the economics of insurance, corporate pension plans, and corporate risk management. Professor Niehaus has won several teaching awards and has co-authored a textbook, *Risk Management and Insurance,* with Scott Harrington.

Karl Perman serves as the director of security for the North American Transmission Forum, where he is responsible for cyber and physical security initiatives. He is also involved with CIP compliance activities. Perman has served in security leadership roles in the electricity and transportation sectors.

J. David Quilter has been recognized as a distinguished leader in law enforcement as well as in private sector asset protection, security program development, and integration for several Fortune 500 corporations over his career. Quilter has developed and designed security processes that help businesses drive productivity and profits in ways that unify security across enterprises big and small. As a security leader Quilter is best known for bringing proven skills, insights, and know-how that advance existing security measures and bridge security gaps while enhancing business operations. Quilter "weaves" together solid security and business practices in ways that deliver safer, more secure operations and enhanced profitability. He is a lifelong learner who continues to serve business and government with distinction. As a leading security consultant Quilter possesses the business savvy and perspective to resolve challenging security, business continuity, and incident management issues. He is author of *From One Winning Career to the Next.*

About Elsevier's Security Executive Council Risk Management Portfolio

Elsevier's Security Executive Council Risk Management Portfolio is the voice of the security leader. It equips executives, practitioners, and educators with research-based, proven information and practical solutions for successful security and risk management programs. This portfolio covers topics in the areas of risk mitigation and assessment, ideation and implementation, and professional development. It brings trusted operational research, risk management advice, tactics, and tools to business professionals. Previously available only to the Security Executive Council community, this content—covering corporate security, enterprise crisis management, global IT security, and more—provides real-world solutions and "how-to" applications. This portfolio enables business and security executives, security practitioners, and educators to implement new physical and digital risk management strategies and build successful security and risk management programs.

Elsevier's Security Executive Council Risk Management Portfolio is a key part of the **Elsevier Risk Management & Security Collection**. The collection provides a complete portfolio of titles for the business executive, practitioner, and educator by bringing together the best imprints in risk management, security leadership, digital forensics, IT security, physical security, homeland security, and emergency management: Syngress, which provides cutting-edge computer and information security material; Butterworth-Heinemann, the premier security, risk management, homeland security, and disaster-preparedness publisher; and Anderson Publishing, a leader in criminal justice publishing for more than 40 years. These imprints, along with the addition of Security Executive Council content, bring the work of highly regarded authors into one prestigious, complete collection.

The Security Executive Council (www.securityexecutivecouncil.com) is a leading problem-solving research and services organization focused

on helping businesses build value while improving their ability to effectively manage and mitigate risk. Drawing on the collective knowledge
of a large community of successful security practitioners, experts, and
strategic alliance partners, the Council develops strategy and insight
and identifies proven practices that cannot be found anywhere else.
Their research, services, and tools are focused on protecting people,
brand, information, physical assets, and the bottom line.

Elsevier (www.elsevier.com) is an international multimedia publishing company that provides world-class information and innovative
solutions tools. It is part of Reed Elsevier, a world-leading provider of
professional information solutions in the science, medical, risk, legal,
and business sectors.

33606913R00080

Made in the USA
Middletown, DE
16 January 2019